P9-DTL-393

In-Line
Roller
Hockey

R

In-Line Roller Hockey

— The Official Guide and Resource Book —

STEVE JOYNER

FOREWORD BY
BRETT HULL

CB

CONTEMPORARY
BOOKS

A TRIBUNE NEW MEDIA COMPANY

Riverside Community College
Library
SEP '96
4800 Magnolia Avenue
Riverside, California 92506

GV 859.7 .J69 1995

Joyner, Steve.

In-line roller hockey

g-in-Publication Data

In-line roller hockey : the official guide and playbook / Steve
Joyner.
     p.   cm.
Includes biographical references and index.
ISBN 0-8092-3448-3
   1. Roller hockey.   I. Title.
GV859.7.J69   1995
796.2'1—dc20   95-9406
                          CIP

All terms mentioned in this book that are known to be trademarks or service marks have been capitalized. Contemporary Books, Inc., cannot attest to the accuracy of this information. Use of a term in this book should not be regarded as affecting the validity of any trademark or service mark.

Rollerblade® is a registered trademark of Rollerblade, Inc., and is used with their permission.

The "NIHA" crest is a trademark of the National In-Line Hockey Association, and is used with their permission.

Cover photographs courtesy of Karhu U.S.A., Inc., Rollerblade, Inc., Ultra-Wheels, and Richard Graham.

All other photographs are by Stephen C. Joyner, except as noted.

Copyright © 1995 by Stephen Christopher Joyner
All rights reserved
Published by Contemporary Books, Inc.
Two Prudential Plaza, Chicago, Illinois 60601-6790
Manufactured in the United States of America
International Standard Book Number: 0-8092-3448-3
10   9   8   7   6   5   4   3   2   1

To all in-line roller hockey players everywhere,
And your love for the game.
Change the world!

For River

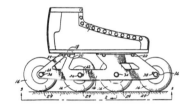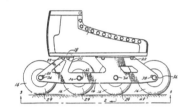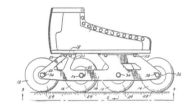

CONTENTS

Foreword by Brett Hull   xi

Acknowledgments   xiii

How to Use This Book   xvii

1 Introduction   1
Answers to Common Questions
What Is In-Line Roller Hockey?
Origins: A Time Line

2 Equipment   19
The In-Line Hockey Skate
The Stick
Protective Equipment
Preplay Equipment Safety Check
Equipment Maintenance
Purchasing Equipment

3 The Rules   **51**
The Rink
Other Areas
Equipment
The Game
The Team
Penalties
Referees

4 Foot Care and First Aid   **77**
Safety Checklist
Foot Care
First Aid

5 Fitness   **93**
Stretching
Stretching Exercises

6 Skills and Drills   **107**
Balance and Stability
Warm-Up Drills
Stopping/Speed Control Techniques
Backward Stopping
Moving Forward
Turning
Backward Skating
Stickhandling
Dribbling Drills
Defensive Stick Checking
Face-Off
Passing and Receiving
Shooting
Goaltending
Goaltending Situations

7 The NIHA   151

What Is the NIHA?
NIHA Alliances and Affiliations
NIHA-Sanctioned Leagues
NIHA Instruction and Clinics
How to Start a League

Glossary   169

Appendix A   183
In-Line Roller Hockey Leagues

Appendix B   185
Organizations and Associations

Appendix C   191
Manufacturers

Appendix D   201
For More Information

Appendix E   211
Bibliography

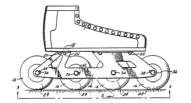 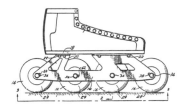 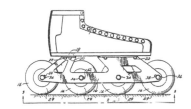

FOREWORD

Hockey is the world's greatest sport, hands down. Whether I'm gunning for an NFL goal-scoring record or lacing up my in-line skates for a pickup game with friends in a parking lot, I just love this game—pure and simple.

Once people *experience* hockey, its appeal is tough to resist. And the tremendous popularity of in-line hockey means that millions more men, women, and children can share my love of the game and experience the thrill of gliding across the rink toward the opposing goaltender, passing, shooting, and scoring! Climate and temperature need no longer prevent you from enjoying this exciting game—with only a pair of skates and proper gear, you can skate almost anywhere.

In-line hockey has become an important part of my off-season exercise and training regimen. It's also great for beginners—organizations such as the National In-Line Hockey Association (NIHA) are standardizing playing rules and developing educational programs designed for novices.

In-line hockey is an ideal sport for conditioning, friendship, and fun. Just remember to always wear full protective gear, play clean, and shoot hard for the corners!

Brett Hull

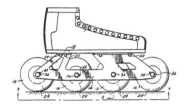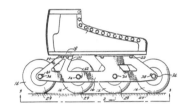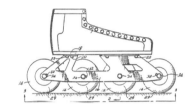

ACKNOWLEDGMENTS

That's my name on the cover, but there would be no book on which to print it if it were not for the combined efforts—large and small—of a lot of people. It is an impossible task to give proper acknowledgment to all the magnificent assistance I have received in preparing this guide, to trace the many valuable suggestions, additions, deletions, and modifications, to give individual thanks for all the photographs and illustrations provided by friends—new and old—by colleagues, manufacturers, and the many individuals dedicated to in-line roller hockey.

But special acknowledgment must go to Joseph R. Mireault and Robert Naegele III, who provided the inspiration and foresight that got this project on its way. Particular acknowledgment must be made to some special people at the NIHA, especially Shawn Jones, who endured endless questions and a few wretchedly hot days in Florida with humor and grace; to Peter Mireault, for wonderful conversation and intelligent editing; to Katina Salafatinos and Berri Goldfarb, for countless favors and assistance; to Richard Graham for always coming through with exceptional photographs and timely information; and to

Scott Wilhite for valued research and assistance in tracing the history of the sport. My personal thanks to Lauren Turetsky and Claude Bossett for the beautiful images they created; to my agent, Christina Brady, and a friend, Anita Diamant; and to my editor, Nancy Crossman, and all at Contemporary Books, for patience, professionalism, and excellence.

And finally, for valued assistance in matters in general, grateful acknowledgment must also be given to Wayne Anderson, Reade Bailey, Doug Balog, Graham Balog, Michelle Barreneche (#98), Todd Bojcun (#3), Graeme Bonar (#29), Dan Bressler, Tony Converse, Kelly Corliss, Peter Davis, Mark Farnen, Stan Fischler, Brady Giroux, Louis Hsiao, Jamie Itagaki, Jim Kirby, Dave Kruse, Chuck Martin, Mark McCreary (#17), Katherine McDonell, Tamara McKernan, Hal Newell, Suzanne Nottingham, Scott Olson, Sam Osborne, Robin Racine, Kyle Ryan (#10), Tom Ryan, Tommy Ryan, Jr. (#2), Jennifer Schwegman, Mike Tomlinson (#14), Henry Zuver III, and others too numerous to mention.

To laugh often and much; to win the respect of intelligent people and the affection of children; to earn the appreciation of honest critics and endure the betrayal of false friends; to appreciate beauty, to find the best in others; to leave the world a bit better, whether by a healthy child, a garden patch or a redeemed social condition; to know that even one life has breathed easier because you have lived. This is to have succeeded.

—*Emerson*

In-line roller hockey is a fast-moving, action sport that poses a continuous risk of personal injury that no type of equipment can ensure against. The author, the National In-line Hockey Association, and Contemporary Books, Inc., recommend that no one participate in this activity unless he or she is a proficient in-line skater, seeks qualified professional instruction or guidance, is knowledgeable of the risks associated with in-line roller hockey, and is willing to personally assume all responsibility associated with those risks. We strongly recommend playing under well-lighted, dry conditions and using quality protective equipment, including a helmet, face mask, mouth guard, gloves, elbow pads, shin guards, and an athletic cup and supporter (for men) or a sports bra (for women). Please skate safely and under control at all times.

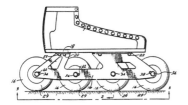 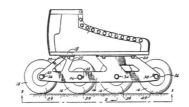 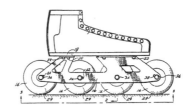

HOW TO USE THIS BOOK

This book employs some special conventions—notes, tips, and cautions—to make it easier for you to get the most out of your in-line roller hockey experience and to quickly find useful information.

Indicates extra information that is not necessarily part of the text but is useful to know in its own right. I often use this to refer you to another part of the book, to clarify a complex issue, or simply to insert information that I think you may like to know.

Alerts you to something extremely important and means that you should stop and pay attention. This is your key to carefully read what is said. Often, I use these labels to indicate items that relate to your personal safety.

Used to draw your attention to special tips or helpful hints that I think will help you better understand a concept, improve your in-line roller hockey skills, or help you get more out of the game.

Gender and Language

Make no mistake—in-line roller hockey is for everyone. *Everyone!* Accordingly, I have made an effort to avoid gender bias whenever possible. Because many team sports, hockey included, have predominantly been a man's domain, some of the sport's less "equitable" terminology has had to be modified. For example, "defensemen" is changed to "defense"; "unsportsmanlike" to "poor conduct," and so on.

However, rather than resort to a cumbersome pronoun combination like "he/she" or "h/er," I have elected to use masculine pronouns in those situations where a pronoun was unavoidable. I did so not out of any sexist leaning, but because it was convenient (just as it was more convenient to use "puck" than "puck/ball").

In-Line Roller Hockey

CHAPTER 1

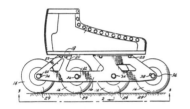 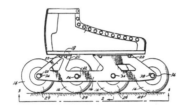 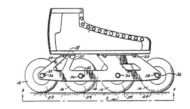

INTRODUCTION

Answers to Common Questions

Q: Where do I start?
A: I don't think you are going to read every page of this book. Well, you may eventually, but this is not exactly a mystery-packed spy novel, is it? It is, however, a guide to help you navigate the world of in-line roller hockey and to help you zero in on what you need during your exploration. Continue to read through these questions and answers. Then turn to the Table of Contents and scan the subentries for specific topics of interest.

Q: For whom is this book written?
A: There's something for just about everyone. Players will find the "Equipment" and "Skills and Drills" chapters especially useful. Coaches, referees, and parents will find specific information about their roles in the game throughout the book. And if you are merely

interested in learning more about the world of in-line roller hockey, this book is for you.

Q: I already know how to play in-line roller hockey. Do I really need this book?
A: Absolutely! This book has something for everyone. In fact, I promise that it will tell you something you never knew before. Watch for the "tips" throughout the book, and be sure to take a look at the book's Appendixes. There you will find lists of resources and lots of other good stuff!

Q: I am brand-new to this sport. Please help. Where do I start?
A: Start by perusing this chapter to get an overview of in-line roller hockey. From there, you have a number of routes to follow. If you are interested in joining a league, see "How to Start a League," Chapter 7. If you need more information on a specific topic, refer to the lists of resources in the Appendixes.

Q: Is this book only for members of the National In-line Hockey Association?
A: Absolutely not. This book will help you whether you are a member or not. If you are interested in becoming a member, see Chapter 7.

Q: I am a skilled in-line hockey player. Where is the good stuff?
A: First, scan through the tips that appear throughout the book. Also, look through "Origins: A Time Line" (in this chapter) for a greater appreciation of the game and how it has evolved. Then go to the Appendixes section at the end of the book.

Q: Is this sport just for the young and nimble?
A: Certainly not. This sport is a great source for fun, fitness, and friendship for anyone—young and old; men and women; girls and boys. The NIHA can help you find league play that is best suited to you.

Q: I'm interested in playing in-line roller hockey. What do I need? How much will it cost? Where do I get it?
A: First of all, and most important, your budget should provide for protective gear. See Chapter 2, "Equipment," for a complete discussion of gear. As for where to get it, refer to Appendix C. The cost? Figure between $200 and $400. As much as half of that will go

"I wanna play."

Courtesy of Richard Graham

toward your skates, the rest for protective gear. And yes, used equipment is available.

Q: I live in Canada. Is this book of any use to me?
A: Absolutely. Specific references to Canada are noted throughout the book. In addition, the lists of resources at the end of the book have numerous Canada-specific entries.

Q: Is in-line roller hockey dangerous? I was wondering because ice hockey is considered a high-risk sport.
A: No! Emphatically, NO! In-line roller hockey is not inherently dangerous. If, however, you play the game in a reckless, careless manner, without proper coaching or a full complement of protective gear, you expose yourself to a greater risk. Under NIHA rules, in-line roller hockey is an incidental (or accidental) contact sport. In other words, "checking," or using the body to intentionally hit an opposing puck carrier by pushing, shoving, or knocking, *is not permitted.*

Q: When does the in-line roller hockey season begin?
A: It has no defined season. With the diversity of climates and playing conditions, in-line roller hockey is a year-round sport. However, NIHA National Championships take place in the fall, with state/provincial and regional competitions in the late-spring and summer months.

Q: I've played ice hockey before. Is in-line roller hockey any different?
A: The short answer is yes, but this question requires a full discussion. This question is addressed in more detail in the first chapter.

What Is In-Line Roller Hockey?

For the most part, in-line roller hockey is the same game as ice hockey, with the following modifications:

- It is played with one fewer skater per team: four skaters and one goaltender per shift. Team rosters usually have no more than 12 players.

- It is played on dry, hard, level, and smooth surfaces. No ice is required.

- The size of the playing surface may vary, within prescribed parameters, depending on the amount of space available at the site (i.e., parking lot, tennis court, "cement-based" ice rinks, and so on). The official size is 180 feet long by 80 feet wide.

- There is no offside penalty. This keeps the game moving more continuously and allows for more playing time.

- There is no checking. Incidental (or accidental) contact is permitted, however.

- Fighting is not tolerated under any circumstances.

- The game may be played with a puck or a ball.

- Protective gear is largely the same, although there are some fundamental differences in design. Generally, in-line roller hockey gear is lighter in weight.

- Tournament and playoff games that are tied at the end of regulation time go into an overtime period of 5 minutes and, if there is still no winner, are decided by a "shoot-out" consisting of four players from each team.

- The game is divided into two halves of play with the option of a) 22-minute straight-time halves or b) 15-minute stop-time periods.

The game of in-line roller hockey is played between boundaries, with the area inside of these boundaries known as a rink, and can be played just about anywhere there is adequate space—indoors or outdoors. Ideally, the dimensions of the rink should be 180 feet long by 80 feet wide, although NIHA rules allow surfaces ranging from as large as 200 feet by 100 feet to 145 feet by 65 feet. The rink should be surrounded by a bordering material—the "structure"—between 8 and 48 inches in height. The surface of the rink is divided into two halves, with a center line 12 inches wide. A 2-foot-diameter circle, placed on the center line, marks the center of the rink. This is where face-offs occur at the beginning of each period and following each goal. In each half of the two zones, there are two additional spots marked at an equal distance from the rink's side border, where other face-offs occur. At either end of the rink are the goals. Each goal is 72 inches wide and 48 inches high, although some latitude is permitted here as well.

An in-line roller hockey game is usually divided into two running-time halves of 22 minutes each. If the score is tied at the game's end, each team is awarded one point in the league standing. There is no overtime play during the regular season. In the case of tournament or league playoffs, an overtime period is played to decide games that are tied after regulation time has expired. Should the game remain tied after the overtime period, a "shoot-out" begins—a one-on-one matchup between a player and the opposing goalie in which the attacking player takes the puck from the center face-off spot and skates toward the goalkeeper in an attempt to score a goal.

In-line roller hockey teams usually carry from 9 to 12 players. Included are at least two forward lines (i.e., a pair of teammates that play together as one offensive unit) and two pairs of defense players, all of whom rotate frequently. Most teams carry two goalkeepers, or goaltenders (usually called goalies), but it is not uncommon for one to play the entire game.

Unlike most other sports, in-line roller hockey does not require that changes in personnel be made only when there is a stoppage in play. Substitutions often occur "on the fly" (i.e., without a stoppage in play). Since play may procced continuously for several minutes, a player may skate over to the team bench just off the playing surface and immediately be replaced by a teammate who plays the same position. The challenge of changing personnel in this way is twofold: it must be done at just the right time, or the opponent will take advantage of the temporary player shortage; and, if confusion occurs upon switching players, a team may end up with too many players on the rink surface and be given a "too many player" penalty. This changing of players can take place only within 10 feet of the bench.

A team's four skaters take positions as forwards or defense. During the course of play, they may move out of position so as to outmaneuver their opponent or as protection against like maneuvers by an opponent. Generally, the two forwards are primarily in an offensive posture. They are usually the first to penetrate into the opponent's defensive zone, and they attempt most of their team's shots on the other team's goal. Forward lines whose members are working well together usually pass the puck back and forth to each other several times until they achieve an opening for a good shot. Although the forwards concentrate on offense, they are also depended on to guard the opposition.

The two defense players typically take a position behind the forwards (i.e., closer to their own goal) and to either side of the goalie. They may become involved directly in their team's offensive mission, but their primary duties are to limit the number of shots on their goal and to break up scoring threats.

As the last line of defense, the goalie is entrusted with keeping the puck from crossing the goal line and entering the goal net. With the goalie stick (which is somewhat wider than the other players' sticks) the goaltender steers the puck to a teammate or away from a foe. The goalie stands in the crease directly in front of the net, always trying to keep an eye on the puck—a task made more difficult when players congregate around the net. Protected by special protective equipment and extra padding, the goalie has to handle all types of shots—short, long, and those from different angles—that hurtle at his body. He may block these with any part of his equipment, or he may glove them and hold on, stopping play. (The goalkeeper is the only player allowed to catch and "freeze" the puck with the catch glove.)

A game starts with a face-off at the center face-off circle. After the puck is dropped by the referee, the opposing players facing off try to gain possession of the puck or direct it to a teammate in a better position. A player for the team in possession of the puck strives for a skating and passing pattern that will avoid losing control and produce the best possible shot on the opponent's goal. The better the shots a team takes, the better its chances of scoring.

In-line roller hockey is one of the few sports in which a team is deprived of a player for an infraction. The most prevalent penalty is the 2-minute minor penalty, which is assessed for rule infractions such as holding, tripping, charging, slashing, and interference. When a referee spots a penalty, the whistle is sounded, play is stopped, and the offender is sent off the rink surface and to the penalty box or bench to serve the penalty.

Major penalties are given for fighting with or injuring an opponent. There are more severe penalties, too. If a player is guilty of insubordination to an official, for example, he receives a 10-minute misconduct penalty. Misconduct suspensions may also be given for use of obscene language—known as the "zero tolerance rule"— prolonged fighting, a second major penalty, or failure to proceed to the penalty box when instructed by an official. When a player is benched for a misconduct or suspended from a game, his team does not play shorthanded. For joining a fight in progress or deliberate intent to injure a player, a player may receive an automatic game misconduct (also called a match penalty), meaning an expulsion from the game.

Origins: A Time Line

c. 4000 B.C. The first wheel is believed to have been invented in ancient Mesopotamia.

c. 2000 B.C. Hockey historians believe that some form of field hockey was played by the Egyptians and the Greeks in modern-day Iran. Other historians have linked hockey with hurling, the Irish game, which is reputed to be the oldest organized stick-and-ball game.

c. 1100 The first ice skates ("scates" in Old English), made of wood and animal bone, are used for transportation over the network of frozen canals that formed "highways" during the winter season. Records and artifacts trace skates to the Netherlands, Scandinavia, and modern-day England.

1527 The word *hockey* first appears in language. Many historians believe that it is from the word *hocquet*, meaning shepherd's crook, that the word *hockey* derived.

1572 First iron ice skates are manufactured. These help reduce the friction between the skate and the ice.

c. 1700 Hans Brinkner designs a pair of roller skates by buckling wooden spools under ordinary boots.

1742 In Edinburgh, Scotland, books of instruction are published and the first ice-skating club, the Skating Club of Edinburgh, is formed. Members later brought skating to Canada, from where it quickly spread to the United States.

1743 The first recorded use of roller skates on the stage, at London's Drury Lane during a play by Tom Hood.

1760 Joseph Merlin, an inventor and musician, comes to London at the behest of the Royal Academy of Sciences to demonstrate his latest invention—the roller skate. Unfortunately, his skates lack steering and braking ability, and, while stringing a violin, he skates through a crystal mirror—smashing both it and roller-skating's popularity to smithereens.

1790   The roller skate makes a comeback when Monsieur van Lede, a French metal maker, introduces the "ground skate," or *patin-a-terre*. This skate later makes a popular, although brief, appearance in Paris and parts of Germany, where it is called "Erdschlittschuh."

1813   Jean Garcin, a French ice-skater and author of "Le Vrai Patineur," unveils a roller skate he calls "Cingar." The Cingar was a simple device made from a wooden board to which rollers were fastened. The unit strapped to the foot. Garcin receives a patent for this skate two years later.

1819   November 12. Monsieur Petibled, a French designer by trade, introduces a roller skate, touted as a dry-land equivalent to the ice skate. The "Petibled," as it is known, is a hardwood plate fitted with three wheels placed in-line. Petibled's high hopes for the skate are ultimately dashed, as turning a corner requires enormous effort.

The "Volito" Skate

1823   April 12. Robert John Tylers introduces the "Volito" skate. It is the first skate on record to use five wheels in a single line—or in-line. The Volito's ability to turn left or right, which it does by using larger center wheels (a form of the wheel "rockering" technique common today), is unprecedented.

1840   In Germany, where roller-skating has been perceived as strictly utilitarian, a clever tavern proprietor thinks to have roller-skating waitresses serve his patrons beer by the bucketloads. Roller-skating, at last, comes to be associated with fun and social occasions.

1849   Roller-skating continues its climb to respectability when it is seen in Giacomo Meyerbeer's esteemed grand opera *The Prophet*. The work had been written to include various ice-skating scenes, including "Les Patineurs," so the composer hired a skilled designer, Louis Legrange, to produce wheeled skates for the performers to use to simulate ice-skating. It works, and the once-ignored device draws large crowds, with as many going to see the roller-skating as to hear the arias.

 To this day, there is still debate as to the precise location of the first games. Kingston, Ontario; Halifax, Nova Scotia; and Montreal, Quebec, each lay claim to having pioneered the sport.

1852   Joseph Gidman of England patents the first roller skate with rubber wheels, known as the "Woodward." This roller skate improves turning ability.

1855   The first organized ice hockey league begins in Kingston, Ontario. It is composed of four teams—the Athletics, the Kingstons, Royal Military College, and Queens University.

1857   Public roller-skating rinks open in Floral Hall at Covent Garden and in Strand, London.

The original Plimpton Skate is on display at the Smithsonian Museum in Washington, D.C.

1863 The Plimpton Skate, designed by one James Plimpton, is introduced. A vast improvement over previous roller-skate designs, this arrangement of four rollers set in pairs, called "trucks," makes roller-skating widely popular. The wheels curve inward, allowing rockering and thus tight turns; hence the nickname "rocking skate." Made of boxwood and fitted with loose ball bearings that increase performance, the skate is the first that can be turned without lifting it off the ground. The design becomes known as the "Circular Running Roller Skate."

The Plimpton Skate (1863)

Available in sizes from 7½ to 11½, the Plimpton Skate sells for $3.00. A roller-skating frenzy ensues in New York, quickly spreads through much of the United States, hops the Atlantic to England, and spreads throughout Europe. Plimpton later founded the New York Roller Skating Association in New York City.

1866 James Plimpton opens the first public roller rink in the world in Newport, Rhode Island, and introduces his "Improved Circular Running Roller Skate."

1875 The first field hockey association is formed, in England. Still, the game struggles to acquire respectability and a unique identity. The main reason appears to be a lack of standardization and rules variation at individual clubs.

1876 Paris inaugurates its first luxurious roller-skating hall, which is closed shortly thereafter when tenants complain. Elsewhere, an artificial ice-skating rink, "Grand Hall Olympia," opens in London. The ice is made by sending a mixture of glycerin and water through copper pipes.

1879 The first codified set of ice hockey rules is established by two students of McGill University (Montreal, Quebec): W. F. Robertson and R. F. Smith. Their rules call for nine players. Refinements quickly follow: the ball is turned into

Elisha Clark Ware,
founder of the
Chicago Roller
Skate Company

a flat disk, the stick is lengthened so it can be held with two hands, the stick's blade is flattened, and the playing surface is reduced by half and enclosed with sideboards.

1884   Levant M. Richardson patents the idea of using steel ball bearings to reduce friction in roller skates. Richardson had founded a huge roller-skate manufacturer, the Richardson Ball Bearing Skate Company, in 1868.

1887   The National Hockey Union, for field hockey, is created at the Clifton Imperial Hotel, England.

The first known ladies' field hockey club is formed. It later becomes known as Molesley.

1890   Five ice hockey teams unite to form the Canadian Amateur Association.

1892   Frederick Arthur, Lord Stanley of Preston, governor-general of Canada, inspired by his two sons' hockey-playing, offers a trophy for the best hockey team in the country, first awarded to the Montrealers a year later. It is the Stanley Cup, today the much-sought-after championship trophy awarded to the best team in the NHL.

1893   Hockey is first played in the United States—at Yale and Johns Hopkins universities.

1904   The International Pro Hockey League forms in Houghton, Michigan. The towns supporting the teams later prove too small to sustain the professionals on a long-term basis.

1905   The Chicago Roller Skate Company is founded by Elisha Clark Ware. The company, pivotal in the roller-skating industry, is later run by his sons: Robert, Ralph, and Walter. In 1937 they support the formation of the Roller Skating Rink Operators Association. In 1955, Ralph Ware is the first person inducted into the roller-skating hall of fame. In 1959, the company starts the Roller Skating Foundation of America in order to promote the sport of roller-skating.

Elsewhere, the Amateur (roller) Hockey Association is founded in England.

1906   The first professional rink (roller) hockey championships take place, in England.

1908   Henry Richardson Plimpton, James Plimpton's son, designs a cup-and-cone device to hold the ball bearings in roller skates. This reduces wheel friction, which increases the efficiency of the roller skate.

1910   The National Hockey Association (NHA) forms.

1913   The Amateur Hockey Association becomes known as the National Rink Hockey Association.

1917   November 26. At the Windsor Hotel in downtown Montreal, the NHL is officially created and the NHA is dissolved. The shake-up is precipitated when the NHA Quebec franchise drops out of the league after having lost too many players to World War I.

1921   The Western Canada Hockey League (WCHL) is created. It is composed of four teams: Regina, Saskatoon, Calgary, and Edmonton.

1924   The first American franchise is granted by the NHL board of governors, and the Boston Bruins are created.

April. The Federation Internationale de Patinage a Roulettes is founded in Montreux. (Note: Later modified to FIRS, or Federation Internationale de Roller Skating, roller-skating's international governing body.)

1925   The WCHL is disbanded and becomes a player feeder for the expanding NHL.

Two four-girl roller hockey teams at Lowe's, Kansas City, Mo., circa 1930

Courtesy of The National Museum of Roller Skating, Lincoln, Neb.

Five-man roller-hockey team with mascot (C.W. Lowe, Jr.)—the Midwest League team champions, 1931

Courtesy of The National Museum of Roller Skating, Lincoln, Neb.

1930s Because of hockey's increasing popularity, the NHL's board of governors decides to make the game more "watchable" for the fans by dividing the rink into three sections, thus making the game faster and higher scoring. Larger rinks are constructed, and corporations begin to sponsor the sport. But the Depression begins to take its toll on hockey: two of the nine NHL teams go bankrupt, and many of the great players are put out to pasture.

1937 The Roller Skating Associations (RSA) is formed. It is composed of the Roller Skating Rink Operators Association, the Roller Skating Manufacturers, the Society of Roller Skating Teachers of America, the Speed Coaches Association, the Roller Hockey Coaches Association, and Proficiency Judges. The organization is founded to serve the needs of the roller-skating industry and to promote roller-skating as a recreational activity.

The United States Amateur Confederation of Roller Skating (USAC/RS) is founded in Detroit, Michigan, as part of the Roller Skating Rink Operators Association. Originally based in Detroit, the organization will move to Lincoln, Nebraska, in 1968.

1966 The Chicago Roller Skate Company patents the "Roller Skate," which provides a "novel skate structure utilizing rollers or wheels, which structure may be adjusted for enabling a skater to simulate ice skates used for one or more activities including racing, hockey and figure skating." Scott Olson, founder of Rollerblade, Inc., would later purchase this patent to develop his original Rollerblade in-line skate.

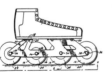

The original Super Sport Skate (U.S. patent 3,880,441), invented by Morris "Maury" Silver, endorsed by Ralph Backstrom, and peddled door-to-door by Scott Olson

1968 January 15. Bill Masterson suffers massive head injuries during an NHL game and dies. Players start wearing protective headgear.

USAC/RS relocates to its present-day location, Lincoln, Nebraska.

1970s Roller-skating's popularity soars.

1973 Following USAC/RS incorporation, roller-skating's popularity increases. The Venice Beach, California, boardwalk, characterized by tube tops, tacky colors, and disco music, will soon become a roller-skater's haven.

1975 Ralph Backstrom (former NHL great and current commissioner of RHI) and Maury Silver (current owner of RHI's Anaheim Bullfrogs) team up to develop the Super Sport Skate, a roller skate. The skates sell for $29.95 a pair.

1979 "The Great Skate Debate," San Francisco, California. Roller-skating reaches its zenith as interest in the skateboard renews. Some 20,000 roller-skaters convene every weekend in Golden Gate Park. Such large numbers wreak havoc on surrounding communities and neighborhoods, resulting in a civic backlash. After months of wrangling, a portion of the park is cordoned off for the skating community.

WHA merges with NHL. By the end of the hockey season, four of the remaining six WHA teams merge with the NHL. The remaining two teams are disbanded, thus ending the WHA.

1981 Scott Olson, a Minneapolis, Minnesota, native, develops an in-line skate based on a 1966 patent. Conceived out of a desire to play ice hockey year-round, his idea led to the birth of Rollerblade, Inc., and with it an industry that has reached nearly a billion dollars in annual retail sales and attracted 14 million U.S. participants in just 14 years.

Courtesy of Scott Olson

Scott Olson

1985 Rollerblade is sold to Robert O. Naegele, Jr.

1987 USAC/RS formally separates from the Roller Skating Rink Operators Association and is recognized as the official national governing body for all competitive roller sports in the United States.

1989 *Speedskating Times* is launched. The nationally distributed periodical features both ice-skating and in-line skating.

Team Rollerblade/Kryptonics is founded. The team tours the country to promote the sport of in-line skating.

1991   In July, the International In-line Skating Association (IISA) is established in a Chicago hotel room.

Inline magazine's premier issue comes out in September. It will become the longest-running nationally distributed periodical to exclusively cover in-line skating and related activities.

1992   *Street Hockey* magazine (renamed *Roller Hockey* magazine in 1994) is launched in September.

At the Summer Olympic Games in Barcelona, Spain, roller hockey is featured as a demonstration sport for the first time in Olympics history.

Roller Hockey Team USA. 1992 Barcelona Summer Olympic Games.[*]

- Ball-and-cane hockey, a brand of roller hockey, was played as a demonstration sport at the Games.

- It took eight years to select the US Roller Hockey Team. A team with ten members went to the Games.

- The competition consisted of twelve teams, including Argentina, Italy, Portugal, and Spain. In these countries roller hockey is second only to soccer in popularity.

- Team USA finished in sixth place overall.

- "You need to set little goals for yourself. If your team finishes in fifth [place], then next time say, 'We'll finish in fourth or third.' Just never quit."

—Dick Chado II, Captain, United States Roller Hockey Team

[*] Jeff Alexander, "Roller Hockey—Olympic Style," *Street Hockey* magazine, May 1993, pp. 36–39.

Roller Hockey International (RHI) is founded by Dennis Murphy, Ralph Backstrom, Alex Bellehumeur, and Larry King.

Two more NHL franchises are added: the Ottawa Senators and the Tampa Bay Lightning.

1993 January. The National In-line Hockey Association (NIHA) is formed in Miami, Florida.

January. The International In-line Skating Association (IISA) is restructured and is moved from Minneapolis, Minnesota, to Atlanta, Georgia.

The World Roller Hockey League (WRHL) is founded by David McLane. The WRHL will later merge with the RHI.

Two more NHL franchises are added: the Anaheim Mighty Ducks and the Miami Panthers.

1994 In November, *NIHA Hockeytalk* magazine is launched. Distribution: members, sponsors, and associates of the NIHA.

Ice hockey is recognized by Sport Canada as an official co-national sport of Canada. Previously, lacrosse was the sole nationally recognized sport.

1995 In October, the NIHA National Championship takes place in Las Vegas, Nevada. Some 100 teams, representing each U.S. state and Canadian province, compete for the National Championship—the "World Series" of amateur in-line roller hockey.

Poetic Just-Ice

In eighteen hundred and sixty-three
A new skate patent had come alive.
Instead of four wheels laid out in a square
Line them all up, and they would slice air.

But rolling along had been a couples affair;
They'd skate at the rink, and preferred to be square.

In nineteen hundred and eighty-five
A few students had started a skate to derive.
Summer street hockey had lost all its charm.
Trip on your shoelaces; fall on your arm.
They needed a surface as smooth as the ice,
Though a skating improvement just might suffice.

But roller skates came in a standardized pair;
All the skates in the world were fact'ry-built, square.

All this square-wheelin' was hard on the feet,
The students' ol' hockey team kept getting beat.
A more fluidic motion had topped their concerns—
What was needed were skates they could put through the turns.

Twist and turns were so sudden; they just couldn't prepare,
And they'd BANG! hit the dirt, cursing skates that were square.

But one summer day, in a student's bright mind,
Popped a perfectly logical skating design.
Better than four-square, this could work fine—
Take the wheels off the sides, and install 'em in a line.
He made up a pair which he strapped to his feet.
The next day at practice he couldn't be beat.

No street hockey players came close to compare,
With wheels laid in a line; theirs were square.

The students had won, they gave up a shout!
Next day the lot of them were all decked out,
In skates that were lighter and faster and turned.
One by one the other teams, lessons were learned,
In gracefully losing to players so fine.
The first men on earth to wear wheels in a line.

The students were asked to make skates by the score,
In a while they really knew they had something there.

Many years have gone by, and a skate revolution,
Laying wheels in a line became the perfect solution.
Engendering health, wearing Lycra in the street,
We strengthen our bodies with wings on our feet.

Roller-skating will never again be unfair,
So good-bye to those skate wheels laid out in a square.
*—Stan O'Connor**

---

*In Stephen C. Joyner, *The Complete Guide and Resource to In-line Skating* (Cincinnati: F & W Publications, 1993).

CHAPTER 2

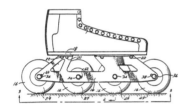
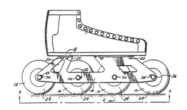
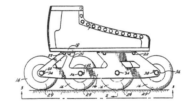

EQUIPMENT

The In-line Hockey Skate

The Wheel

Deceptively simple and ever so common, the wheel is easy to take for granted. We have all seen them. We know what they do. Roll, right? So what's the big deal?

The eight (or six) wheels that are underneath your skates are, collectively, the most critical component of any in-line hockey equipment that you buy—and, considering their frequency of replacement, probably the most expensive. In-line skate wheels look like a row of plastic doughnuts standing at attention. And as any good baker will tell you, the secret to the best baked goods is in the recipe. Wheel designers, bakers of a different sort, use similar processes of mixing and heating various resins and ingredients that make their "doughnuts" unique and special in every way.

In-line wheels are made of polyurethane, a type of plastic with special chemical properties that make it an ideal

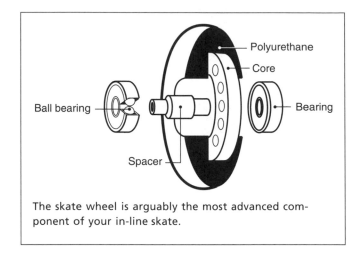

The skate wheel is arguably the most advanced component of your in-line skate.

compound for in-line wheels. Beyond the material itself, a wheel's performance properties are determined by a number of constants (wheel characteristics) and variables (skater characteristics).

The constants include the wheel's size (or diameter), durometer (or hardness), rebound (ability to absorb energy), profile (or radius), and core (the center plastic-like area that holds the bearings in place). The variables pertain to you, the in-line roller hockey player: your body weight, your skating style (speed, recreational, in-line roller hockey, etc.), your braking technique, the climate where you skate, and the play surface (wood, asphalt, Sport Court™ surface, etc.).

By considering all of these factors, and doing a bit of your own research (reading this book, talking to other skaters, and so on), you should get more for your money the next time you purchase a set of wheels. An understanding of how the wheel works and how it can help you be the best player you can be is instructive.

Size

The size, or diameter, of an in-line wheel is how tall the wheel is. The outside diameter, or "OD," of the running surface is measured in millimeters (mm). While small wheels turn and accelerate more quickly than large wheels, large wheels require more energy to "spool up" to higher RPMs (revolutions per minute), but tend to be more stable at higher speeds. Wheel sizes range from 52 mm for aggressive street and so-called extreme skating to 64 mm for children and goalies and 82 mm for speed skating. Most recreational wheels are

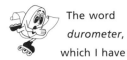 The word *durometer*, which I have just defined as a measuring tool, is often used interchangeably with the word *hardness*, as in "The wheel's durometer (or 'hardness') allowed for a tight, controlled turn."

between 70 mm and 72.5 mm. Hockey wheels are typically between 72 mm and 76 mm.

Durometer (Hardness)

The hardness of plastic materials is measured with a tool called a durometer.

There are several scales of measurement, with the "A" scale used primarily for wheels (e.g., "78A"). The actual hardness of the wheel is rated from 1 (no resistance to applied pressure) to 100 (extremely hard plastic). So a 74A wheel is softer than a 93A wheel.

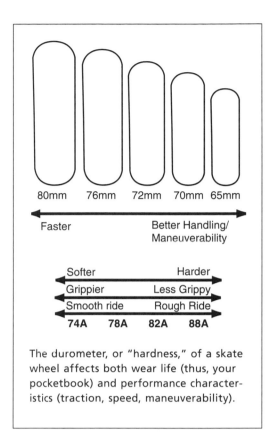

The durometer, or "hardness," of a skate wheel affects both wear life (thus, your pocketbook) and performance characteristics (traction, speed, maneuverability).

Durometer affects wear life, shock absorption, traction, and, in most cases, rebound. The durometer of most in-line wheels ranges from 74A (soft) to 93A (hard). Soft wheels provide more traction, have a smoother ride, return more energy when compressed (rebound), but have only average wear-life. Contrarily, hard wheels slide more, are less shock absorbent, but last longer. Although in-line roller hockey played on asphalt or concrete generally calls for a softer wheel (84A, for example), for better shock absorption over cracks and pebbles, larger players may actually need a harder wheel, since their body weight compresses a soft wheel too much, increasing the "footprint" of the wheel and thus slowing the skater down.

Durometer may also be considered as a measure of a wheel's durability. This is easy to understand. All things being equal, a softer wheel is going to wear down more quickly than a harder wheel. Fortunately, a wheel's wear-life can be lengthened by properly flipping and rotating skate wheels (see discussion of wheel maintenance later in this chapter). If you want to save your wheels and your money, get into the habit of doing this.

Rebound

Rebound is the amount of energy a wheel returns when it is compressed. As a wheel is pushed into the ground by the skater's weight and turning force (torque), it absorbs energy. When this energy is released, the wheel rebounds, and you benefit by getting a little more "zing" out of each stride. So, all else being equal, high-rebound wheels are faster and livelier, while low-rebound wheels are slower and feel a bit flat.

Unfortunately, there is no scale to measure rebound. In-line hockey players and wheel experts resort to dropping wheels on the ground or biting them with their teeth to determine their rebound. Compared with durometer and diameter measurements, it is a crude method, but it does the job.

Core

A wheel's core (or hub) is the part of the wheel around which the meat of the wheel (the polyurethane) is molded. It is also the part of the wheel that holds the bearings in place. The core is usually made from a stiff thermoplastic nylon that keeps it from flexing under the pressure of skating.

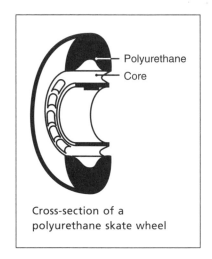

Cross-section of a polyurethane skate wheel

Cores are either closed, with no visible spokes, or open, with an assortment of spoke or hole designs. The sides of less-expensive wheels are covered with urethane. On more expensive wheels, however, the core may occupy upward of 50 percent of the diameter, thus reducing the weight of the wheel. An open-core wheel also dissipates excessive heat generated by inefficient bearings or by a wheel's spinning so fast that the bearings overheat, which can lead to wheel meltdown—the same as experiencing tire blowout on the highway.

Profile

The profile of a wheel is the outline, or sidecut, of the rolling surface. It tells you how much polyurethane is in contact with the skating surface. Think of it as the "footprint" your wheel leaves on the

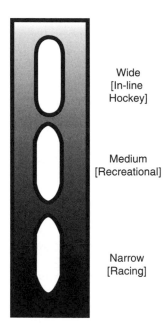

Wide
[In-line
Hockey]

Medium
[Recreational]

Narrow
[Racing]

Wheel Width
Comparison

Polyurethane skate
wheels have different
widths, or profiles,
depending on the type
of surface or the kind
of skating you do.

ground. A wider, more rounded profile improves traction and maneuverability, but tends to be slower. This profile is best suited for in-line roller hockey. Wheels with a narrower profile (smaller radius), however, are faster, since there is less resistance. Small-radius wheels have a narrow profile and are faster than large-radius, or wide-profile, wheels.

Axles

Axles come in two varieties: bolt-and-nut (protruding), and axle tube and screw (flush). Most high-end (more expensive) in-line roller hockey skates use the axle tube and screw.

Spacers

The spacer, usually made of plastic or metal, is a small part that separates the two bearings inset in the wheel's core.

Bearings

It takes effort to skate. Bearings help us get the most out of our efforts. They help to maximize wheel spin and the push forces a skater can produce. Each wheel turns on two cartridge bearings containing metal ball bearings that are protected from outside contaminants by thin-walled seals. Bearings are lubricated with either grease or oil, depending on the manufacturer. Typically, sealed bearings are prepacked in grease. Serviceable (or unsealed) bearings are lubricated with oil.

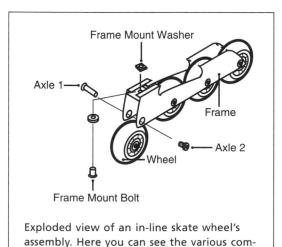

Exploded view of an in-line skate wheel's assembly. Here you can see the various component parts of the wheel.

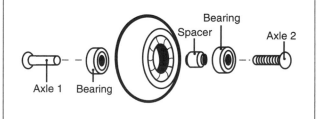

This diagram shows how all the pieces of the skate frame and wheels fit together.

 Increasingly, in-line skate manufacturers are designing boots (and other equipment) tailored to women. Among the most important modifications are to the "last" of the boot—that is, the molded contour of the inner boot. In simple terms, this means greater support and comfort.

Bearings are rated on an internationally recognized quality scale called ABEC (Annular Bearing Engineering Council). Generally, the higher the rating, the faster the bearing. Bearings for in-line skates are rated on the so-called Shore "A" ABEC scale and typically range from 1 to 5 (odd numbers only). For instance, ABEC 1 bearings offer most skaters adequate speed and life span, and are regarded as the standard for in-line use. ABEC 3 bearings are popular for those skaters interested in more speed, although they are not necessarily longer lasting. Bearings rated below ABEC 1 are called "semiprecision" or "unground precision." A rating of ABEC 5 or above is considered "super precision" and is really more bearing than you need to play in-line roller hockey.

Bearings come in both shielded and unshielded varieties. Shielded bearings are permanently sealed. Typically, they are packed in grease, are less expensive than unshielded bearings, but are more difficult to service. Most factory in-line skates come with shielded bearings.

Unshielded bearings are not permanently sealed. They are more expensive than their shielded counterparts, but are easier to clean, since they have removable rubber seals. If you become serious about in-line roller hockey, you may want to consider investing in an unshielded bearing kit.

The Boot

Materials

The boot of your in-line roller hockey skate is probably made of leather or molded plastic. Whatever the material, the boot should be flexible when you bend your knees, but fairly rigid laterally. Different boot materials have different features:

Leather and Like Materials

- More expensive.

- Need break-in time.

- Do not breathe as well as some molded boots.

- May require air-circulation torque.

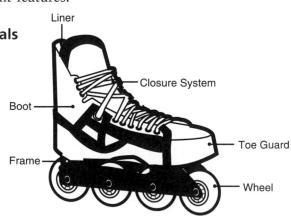

Young in-line roller hockey players and parents: I know that room for growth must be allowed. To be sure, in-line hockey skates are an investment, but please *do not* fit too large. Even with several pairs of thick socks, the boot just will not be able to adequately support the ankle from the significant tension placed on it during playing conditions. The most growth allowance you should make is about a thumb's width behind the heel when the foot is pushed forward as far as it will go in an unlaced boot. Also, when buying skates, wait until just before the season begins. Otherwise, you may find yourself having to upgrade to a larger size before the season ends.

Molded Plastic

- Less expensive.

- Memory form (footbed that molds to the contours of the foot).

- Removable liner (for easier cleaning).

- Tend to offer greater breathability than leather boots.

Proper Fit

Every player has a personal preference that must be considered. However, skates are constructed to meet the foot's requirements, and an improperly fitted skate can result in premature breakdown of the boot, and more important, "breakdown" of your foot. Generally, a stitched skate (i.e., leather or nylon) will fit from one to one-and-a-half sizes down from your regular shoe size. Molded boots, however, generally fit the same as your regular shoe size. Fitting gauges, such as the Mondo Point system (a universally recognized sizing scale based on the length of the foot in centimeters), indicate only approximate sizing and should not be considered as a true fit. For the best fit, try on a few different sizes and walk around in them.

1. While sitting down, put the skate on and immediately kick the heel back to the rear of the boot. You should be able to spread open your toes in the toe cap. They should not be crushed or curled up against the boot.

2. Lace up the boot while continuously kicking the heel back. This ensures that the lacing is being tightened evenly from the bottom to the top. The lacing tension should be firm, but not so tight that blood circulation in the foot is affected. Think "snug" fit. Too loose or too tight is no good.

3. After the boot is completely laced, walk—or waddle, if you will—around the store. The rear area of the foot should feel snug and secure, with no movement or slipping. The foot should rest comfortably on the footbed. The toes should extend flat within the toe cap. Before you make a final decision, remove the boots, browse around the store for a few minutes, and put them back on for final consideration.

Lace-up boots, common on most in-line roller hockey skates, allow you to improve the comfort and fit by adjusting the tension of the laces.

Special Features

Manufacturers of in-line roller skates offer a variety of special features that improve the performance and durability of skates.

Toe Cap

Usually molded of polyethylene (plastic), the toe cap provides protection from impact and abrasion. Some are removable and replaceable when they show excessive wear.

Support Strap

Support straps are used around the ankle portion of the boot to provide additional lateral (side-to-side) support.

Heel Stabilizer (Molded Heel)

A heel stabilizer, or molded heel, provides solid support in the wheel portion of the boot. It also protects the heel from direct blows by a puck, skate, or stick.

Air Circulation

There are a variety of ways for a manufacturer to increase the air circulation and breathability of a skate boot. Look for air-intake slits on the sides of the boot; a breathable liner; and a tongue that allows air to circulate in the boot.

Liner

Some boots have a removable liner, sort of a boot within a boot, that can be aired out, helping to keep the boots clean and dry. Most leather boots, however, have permanent liners made of leather, foam, or nylon.

Laces

Most in-line roller hockey skates use a lace-up closure system, as opposed to the microadjustable buckles found on most recreational

 Another option is to use two or three separate laces on each skate, tying each one to the desired degree of tightness.

After-market support straps can add lateral support to the boot. Rollerblade, Inc., makes Power Straps, which are effective and easy to use.

skates. Although there is no such thing as a perfect fit, creative lacing (i.e., tight and low, loose in the middle, tight and high) can help.

Frame

The frame of the skate is what holds the wheels in place; it connects to the underside of the boot. Frames are generally made of nylon, aluminum, or a composite (combination) material. Your choice of frame material should be determined by your level of play and commitment to the sport, since there are wide variations in the cost of materials.

Nylon

Most less-expensive frames are made of a glass-reinforced nylon. This type of frame is more flexible and less stable than aluminum or composite frames. However, nylon frames tend to reduce the overall cost of the skate and are quite capable of holding up to the rigors of in-line roller hockey. This is a good choice for the player who is just starting out or who is still growing.

Aluminum

An aluminum frame is stronger and lighter than a nylon frame. As you might expect, it warrants a higher price.

Composite

Theoretically, you could spend a bundle of money and have a titanium (an extremely strong, lightweight metal) frame made. But will it make you a better in-line roller hockey player? Probably not.

Other Skate Considerations

Wheel Compatibility

In addition to the material used in the frame, you should be aware of how large a wheel can be accommodated by the frame. Some frames are limited to wheel sizes in the low 70s (millimeters). If you think you might like to use your skates for activities besides hockey, you should inquire about this.

Rockering

Rockering (using wheels of different sizes) increases a skater's maneuverability by effectively creating a "curved" wheel base. In other words, since there are fewer wheels in contact with the surface, there is less wheel-to-surface resistance to overcome. (Professional dancers know this concept. That's why they spin on the toes of their feet, not the soles.) However, rockering also reduces the stability of the skate, since there are fewer wheels in contact with the surface at any one time. Therefore, only a skilled in-line roller hockey player should consider rockering.

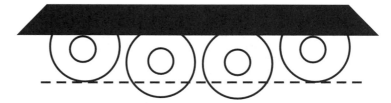

This diagram shows a so-called rockered skate, otherwise known as rockering.

Skates that feature "built-in" rockering have oval spacers in the two middle wheel axles that can be flipped so as to lower the wheels relative to the front and rear wheels.

Rockering can also be achieved by using two larger-diameter wheels in the middle (or smaller wheels on the ends), with at least a 4-mm difference in the diameter. For instance, if your wheels are 72 mm, replace the two middle wheels with 76-mm wheels, and if your wheels are 76 mm, replace the front and rear wheels with 72-mm wheels.

Cantering

Cantering is the process of laterally adjusting the angle of the wheel base. Many professional ice hockey players canter their skate blades to improve performance. Moving the front blade mounting inward changes the blade angle, thus providing a longer stride.

Some in-line roller hockey skates offer this toe-in/toe-out adjustment feature. If your skating fundamentals are sound, you may want to experiment with cantering.

Cantering Technique

1. Remove the wheels that interfere with access to the frame mounting screws.

2. Loosen, but do not remove, both the front and rear frame mounting screws, using a T-handle wrench. (One is usually provided with your skates.)

3. Pivot the front of the frame laterally toward the instep of the boot.

4. Tighten the front and rear frame mounting screws.

5. Reattach the wheels. Make sure the axles are snug, but not too tight.

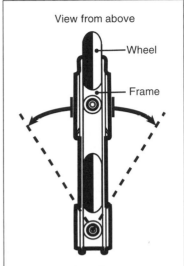

View from above

Wheel

Frame

Cantering is a skate adjustment that laterally changes the angle of the wheel base. Some skaters canter their skates to help maximize the efficiency of their skating strides.

Try a few different angles before determining your permanent frame position. This is strictly a matter of preference. If it feels right for you, go with it.

The Stick

Over the past decade, hockey sticks have undergone a revolution all their own. As the sport has taken on a greater following, equipment manufacturers have responded with greater variety. There is good and bad news.

The good news is that strength and performance have improved enormously. The bad news is that the choices seem limitless, and determining what is best for you can boggle the mind.

To simplify this process, let's look at each component of the hockey stick itself. This will help you in narrowing your choices.

Shaft

Currently, there are three basic types of shafts on the market.

Wood

Wood has been the main component of sticks since hockey was invented. While manufacturing technology has progressed, many players find that wood still gives them the best "feel" for the puck. Wood is still used by manufacturers to varying degrees in most street- and ice-hockey sticks.

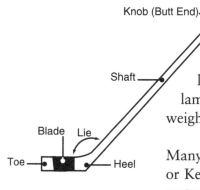

The hockey stick

Wood sticks are made of compressed strips of wood called laminates that are bound together by resins. The number of laminations and their individual thickness determines the overall weight, thickness, flexibility, and durability of the stick's shaft.

Many traditional wood sticks are reinforced with fiberglass, graphite, or Kevlar to increase strength. Typically, manufacturers apply these materials on the outside of the stick and/or between the wood laminations, thereby making the shaft stiffer and more durable.

The amount of flexibility, or "flex," in your shaft affects your performance as a player. Shafts made of wood have greater flexibility than those made of aluminum. For children and players with marginal strength, this is something worth considering, since the whip action of a stick with greater flex will generate a more forceful shot. Contrarily, flex becomes a liability for a physically strong player, since the blade trails behind the power point of a shot.

Ultimately, how much flex you should have in your stick depends on your personal preference. Some players find that firm sticks are better for controlling the puck, while others prefer a stick with plenty of flex. Experiment with different sticks to determine what feels right for you.

Aluminum

Hockey was changed forever with the introduction of the aluminum stick. Aluminum provides greater stiffness in the stick and weighs less than wood.

Aluminum sticks are made of either 6,000 or 7,000 series aluminum (7,000 series aluminum is used in the manufacture of aircraft). While wood fatigues and develops more flex over time, the amount of flex in aluminum is set when it is made.

Graphite and Composites

Composite sticks are made of two or more materials, such as graphite and Kevlar. Like many other composite products on the market—from sauté pans to motorcycle frames—these sticks are greater (i.e., stronger and lighter) than the sum of their parts. And they are always more expensive.

In the final analysis, your choice of materials should be based on how important the game becomes to you. You can find an old wooden hockey stick at a flea market for $10 or you can spend hundreds on a custom-made composite stick.

Blade

Lie

Lie is a measure of the angle the shaft makes with the blade. The smaller the angle, the greater the lie number.

To determine your proper lie, get in your basic in-line roller hockey stance, holding the stick in front of you. If the toe of the stick's blade is not in contact with the surface, you need a lower-numbered lie.

 Smaller players will probably need to cut a few inches off the stick's end (or knob). Also, when selecting a stick, it is better to buy one that is too big than too small. You can always cut it down to size.

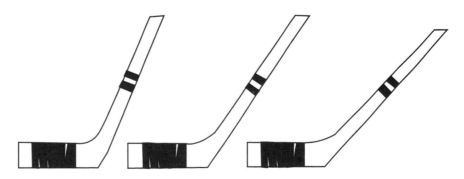

Three sticks showing three different lies. The stick lie is determined by measuring the angle of the blade and the shaft.

 Sticks without a curved blade do not have a handedness label and are suitable for either left- or right-handed players.

Lie can also be determined by observing the skating style of an in-line roller hockey player. If you skate low (more bent over) to the surface, you will probably want a lower lie—say, 3 or 5. Especially tall players will use a higher lie (6 or 7). The most common lies are somewhere in the middle of these extremes, about 5 or 6.

Curvature

There are two types of blade curves, the midcurve and the heel curve. The midcurve begins at the midpoint of the blade. This blade style helps generate extra "snap" for shooting. The heel curve has a greater arc than the midcurve and is the more popular of the two, since greater arc makes it easier to stick-handle the puck.

Length

To size your stick properly, place the end of the stick's blade on the surface. The knob of the stick should come up to between your chin and nose.

To measure for your proper stick length, make sure you are wearing your skates. Place the toe of the stick's blade on the surface between your skates. The stick should come up to between your chin and nose. (Most players prefer it to be closer to their nose than chin.)

Handedness

Sticks with curved blades are labeled either "L" (left) or "R" (right). Since many sticks and hockey players come out of French-speaking Canada, a stick may also be labeled "G" (gauche/left) or "D" (droit/right). Some sticks may use both designations—"R/D" (right/droit), for example.

Courtesy of Karhu USA, Inc.

In-line roller hockey equipment. Clockwise from center: shin guards, girdle (optional), gloves, stick, elbow pads, and shoulder pads (optional).

Protective Equipment

Shoulder Pads

To properly size shoulder pads, measure your chest just below the armpits. Shoulder pads should fit snugly, and the vital tips of the pads should be properly positioned under the shoulders. The biceps pads should not interfere with the elbow pads.

When an in-line roller hockey player loads up with shoulder pads he looks like something akin to Robocop. And with the look comes an attitude and a feeling of invulnerability. Players who are not similarly outfitted are more likely to be injured by players who wear the pads. The bottom line? Make the game safer, less expensive, and more fun for everyone by leaving the shoulder pads on the store rack.

 Youth (non-adult) players: because in-line roller hockey is an incidental (unintentional) contact sport, shoulder pads are not necessary. In fact, all things considered, it may be safer not to wear them.

Elbow Pads

The elbow pad protects the elbow from bruises and road rash ("raspberries"). It should be fitted by measuring the length between the middle of the biceps and the cuff of the glove—usually about the midpoint of the forearm. If you wear a short-cuff glove, use a longer-model elbow pad.

Gloves

Gloves are sold with both S-M-L and inch-length size designations. For the latter, measure the length between the middle of your biceps and the cuff of the glove. When the glove is fastened securely there should be no gap between the pad and the cuff of your glove. Players who wear a short-cuff glove should choose a longer elbow pad so that the arm is protected from fingertip to just below the shoulder.

The glove's thumb should be protective and flexible; the glove's foam padding dense. Gloves should not be so large that they will inhibit your ability to properly feel the stick or so small as to jam your fingertips.

Hockey Pants

Hockey pants are worn to protect the hip, thighs, kidneys, and tailbone from body bruises and road rash. The pants are typically made of a nylon lining covering a molded polyethylene (i.e., foam) and are secured to the body with a belt and drawstring. The pants should reach the top of the knees and extend upward to cover the critical areas. Hockey pants are sized according to waist size.

Shin Guards

The hockey girdle, which looks like a protective bodysuit and extends from the lower rib cage down to the top of the knee, is not necessary for recreational in-line roller hockey.

Shin guards are sold with both S-M-L-XL and inch-length size designations. For the latter, measure from the center of the knee to the top of the skate boot. Shin guards that are too long will ride up the leg so that the cap is actually several inches above the knee, offering little or no protection. For those shin pads without built-in elastic or Velcro straps, use special shin guard straps and/or plenty of tape to hold the pads in place.

A coach is helping his player by securing shin guards with tape.

Helmet

You may want to see if your helmet has been approved by either HECC (Hockey Equipment Certification Committee) or its Canadian counterpart, CSA (Canadian Safety Association).

The helmet protects your head from falls and incidental blows. Position the helmet on your head so the rim is just above the eyebrow. If necessary, gradually downsize the helmet until a comfortable, snug fit is achieved. Tighten and secure the helmet straps. The helmet should be snug enough so that it does not rotate. *Never* wear an oversized helmet.

Face Guard ("Mask" or "Cage")

The face guard should fit snugly to the chin. If it is too long, it may come into contact with the nose or mouth. With your mouth closed, the chin should fit comfortably into the chin cup. Attach the face guard securely to the helmet according to the instructions provided. Face guards must meet CSA (Canadian) or HECC (U.S.) and American Society for Testing Materials (ASTM) standards, and must be approved for use with the helmets to which they are attached.

Mouthpiece

 For those who wear braces or other dental appliances, Shock Doctor by EZ Guard has a special mouth-guard application.

The use of internal mouth guards greatly reduces the risk of brain concussions, jaw injuries, chipped teeth, and oral cuts. The mouth guard comes in several standard sizes and often comes with a special sizing kit so it will conform to the "bite" of your mouth. When shopping for a mouth guard, look for these features: contoured "ribs" that mold to the front teeth, built-in shock-absorbing pads for the back of the mouth, and a quick-release strap for efficient removal in an emergency.

Undergear

Support Shorts (or Strap) and Cup

Wearing a protective cup and supporter is essential in in-line roller hockey. Thanks to special shorts, the cup can be positioned into a built-in pouch, thus eliminating the less-comfortable cup support (i.e., "jock strap"). Whichever method is used, try to get a cup designed specifically for hockey—they are a bit larger and stronger. Sizing: boys' and standard men's sizes.

Because of the nature of their position, goalies must wear a special, highly protective cup. The goalie cup—actually a cup and supporter in a combined unit—looks something like brief-styled underwear on steroids. The higher-end models are deeply padded with polyethylene foam; some actually have special air pockets for greater impact cushioning. Sizing: adjust to fit.

Sports Bra and Pelvic Protector

There are a few pieces of protective equipment designed for the woman player.

Some women should wear a sports bra. (If you need to ask, you are probably not ready for one yet.) The sports bra redistributes the breast mass across the chest wall, and thus helps to reduce breast motion to a safe and comfortable range.

A sports bra should suit your bust size and the substantial amount of motion inherent in in-line roller hockey.

The pelvic protector is designed to fit the unique contours of a woman's body, without chafing. Sizing: standard waist measurements.

Goalie Gear

Catch Glove

 Remove all gear from your hockey bag after returning home from each game or practice. Your (sweaty) gear will dry faster, which will make it last longer.

As the name implies, the goalie catch glove, or mitt, is used to catch the puck. It has a wide, durable cuff that extends up the wrist several inches. Ideally, a glove should be selected based on whether you play with a true puck or a ball. The glove for catching balls has a deep well pocket, like that found in a baseball glove. The glove for pucks is shallower and has a reinforced pouch. You should select the biggest glove that you can control and hold up steadily.

Blocker

Sometimes referred to as a "waffle," a blocker is worn on the opposite hand to the catch mitt (i.e., the stick hand), and is filled with high-density padding to cushion the puck. It is held with a padded, precurved inner glove that is molded to the back of the blocker and (usually) secured with a Velcro strap. The front surface is slightly curved to help redirect shots. Weight is especially important in selecting a blocker—remember, you have to hold and control a stick with that same hand.

Goalie Pants

Goalie pants are heavily padded shorts that disperse the impact of a shot and protect the hip, thigh, and tailbone. Consider goalie pants with removable pads; they are easier to clean.

Leg Pads

Goalie leg pads are the largest and most distinctive protective equipment a goaltender wears. Each pad is made specifically for either the left or right leg. Goalie leg pads have evolved to the point where they are extremely light, durable, and water resistant, and have excellent shock-absorption characteristics.

The bad news is that they are very expensive—quite possibly as expensive as all the other protective gear combined. However, they should last a lifetime with proper care, and they have excellent resale value should you trade up or abandon the sport altogether.

Goalie Helmet and Mask

 Sometimes you will come across a mask, helmet, or goalie helmet that has not yet been approved by the two certifying bodies that test protective hockey equipment: HECC and CSA. Look for the words "CSA- and HECC-approval pending" or "Pending CSA and HECC approval."

The goalie helmet and mask can be purchased as one integrated unit or separately. The combination helmet and mask should fit so that it does not obstruct your peripheral vision or rotate when fastened. An oversized helmet can cause serious injury and should *never* be used.

For any piece of protective equipment to be as effective as possible, it should be worn as designed. Make sure the helmet's chin strap is fastened at all times.

Mouthpiece

Like all other in-line roller hockey players, a goalie must wear a mouthpiece.

Preplay Equipment Safety Check

The last thing an in-line roller hockey player wants to worry about is if his equipment is going to perform as designed. To reduce that worry, use the following equipment checklist prior to each game and practice.

Skates

- Check your wheels for wear and tightness. Are the wheels suitable for the surface type?

- Store a replacement set of wheels in your equipment bag.

- Bearings should be clean and free of dirt.

- Check laces for cuts or frays. Keep an extra pair in your equipment bag.

- Check boots for broken eyelets, buckles, tongue, and frame.

Shin Pads/Goalkeeper Leg Pads

- Leg straps should be securely fastened.

- Check for cuts, frays, cracks, or worn spots.

- Keep extra straps/fasteners in equipment bag.

Hockey Pants

- Check for missing pads in the pants and tears in the pockets that may cause the pads to slip out.

- Make sure that buckles operate effectively.

- Protective cup should be checked for damage.

Gloves

- The palm of the glove should be secure to the fingers so that no part of the hand is exposed (i.e., worn holes in the glove, stitching that has come apart from the fingers, etc.).

- If gloves are leather, oil the palms. If they are worn down, patch or replace.

- Laces or Velcro straps should be examined for cuts and frays on the cuff.

- Goaltender's catch glove should be checked for cuts in the pocket.

Elbow Pads/Goalkeeper Arm Pad

- The straps that secure elbow pads and goalkeeper arm pads should be checked for damage. The Velcro material found in most pads should be cleaned of "fuzzy" debris so it will fasten securely.

- Check that the elbow pad shells are properly affixed to the elbow pads.

Goalkeeper Chest Pad

- Check to see that the chest pad buckle latches properly.

- Straps should be checked for cuts and frays.

Helmet

- Check for loose rivets, screws, snaps, or bolts.

- Wash the interior with mild soap and a damp cloth periodically.

- Straps should be checked for cuts, frays, and fastening ability.

- The padding of the helmet should be examined for proper fit and placement.

Face Mask

 If you wear braces or another dental appliance, be especially careful when fitting and applying the mouthpiece. If in doubt, speak to your dentist and/or orthodontist.

- Check for defects, such as a bent cage or cracked shield.

- Make sure the shield is properly fitted to the helmet.

Mouthpiece

- Make sure that there are no rough edges that may cut the mouth or damage the teeth.

- Keep your mouth guard clean and in its protective case when not in use.

- Wash thoroughly before and after each game and practice.

Sticks

Some players choose not to tape their hockey sticks. Also, tape mars some surfaces and is not allowed to be used at some facilities.

- Examine your hockey stick for chips, cracks, and splinters that may cause breakage during play. Keep at least one extra stick on hand in case your stick breaks.

- Sticks should be both properly measured and taped before play.

Equipment Maintenance

Rotating and Repositioning Wheels

Wheels of any hardness (durometer) will wear out with use. Once you have acquired all of your in-line roller hockey gear, replacing worn-out wheels will be your largest maintenance expense. Proper wheel rotation is essential to preserving your cash and extending the lifetime of your wheels. Your wheels should be rotated on a regular basis, or whenever wear is apparent.

The rate of wheel wear is determined by a combination of factors:

- The weight of the skater.

- Skating style.

- The abrasives of the skating surface.

- The climate of your skating area. Heat accelerates the breakdown of wheels.

- Frequency of wheel rotation.

- Use a small vacuum cleaner after each use to keep your skate wheels and chassis free of dirt.
- Cover your skate wheel and chassis after each use. ProLine Covers is a product that keeps skate wheels clean and protected. See resource list for more information.
- Monitor wear on inner edges of wheels. After a few hard power slides, it may be time to rotate.
- You may want to do all your maintenance at one time. If so, see "Cleaning Bearings" below.

Tools You Will Need

- Crescent wrench (socket wrench) and Allen wrench(es). (Usually supplied by skate manufacturer.)

- Rag or paper towels.

- Small parts brush.

Technique

1. While sitting, nestle boot upside-down in between your legs. (Skate stands also work well.)

2. Remove all wheels from the frame by unscrewing the axle screws with wrenches.

3. Rotate wheels as shown in figure. (This one-step process both rotates and repositions wheels.)

4. Reassemble axles and tighten. Be careful—overtightening can decrease performance and damage bearings.

5. Spin each wheel. If they do not all downspin for the same amount of time, adjust tightness of axle screws.

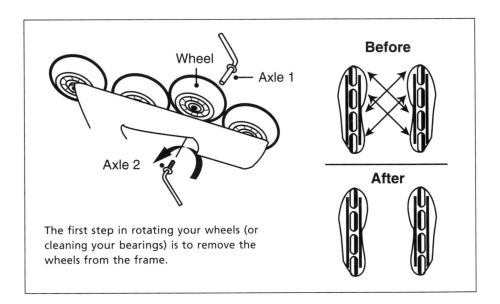

The first step in rotating your wheels (or cleaning your bearings) is to remove the wheels from the frame.

Cleaning Bearings

Nestled into each skate wheel's core is a pair of bearings. They are separated by a plastic or metal spacer (or "bushing"). Within each bearing are small steel balls that roll around on an inner track called a "race." When dirt and moisture get into the bearing, the efficiency of the ball bearings is reduced. In other words, when they slow down, you slow down.

- When cleaning bearings, avoid flammable and/or toxic solvents if possible. (Try non-toxic, citrus-based Black Hole Bearing Cleaner.)

- If you would prefer not cleaning your bearings yourself, call your local skate shop to see if they offer this service. However, it is a good idea to clean them yourself at least once. It helps you better understand what they do and how they work.

- Use a hair dryer to expedite the drying process.

There are two types of bearings that you should know about: sealed and unsealed. A sealed bearing means a bearing shield is permanently closed. To open it, you must literally pry open and destroy one of the shields. Since bearing shields are made of thin metal, they are not too difficult to remove with the proper technique. Once the shield is removed it can be left "exposed," or an after-market rubber seal may be pressed into place to keep dirt out.

Unsealed bearings have a reusable rubber shield on one side; the other side is permanently sealed. Although unsealed bearings are easier to maintain, they tend to be more expensive.

Some signs that indicate your bearings need to be cleaned are the following:

- Gritty, dry sound.

- Wheel vibrations.

- Wheels don't spin freely or equally.

- Dirt is visible.

What You Will Need

- A clean work surface and a ventilated working area.

- Paper towels or cloth rags.

- Small, shallow glass or metal container (old pie tins, 36-mm-film containers, and coffee cans work well).

- Cleaning solution (solvents; mineral spirits).

- Lubricating oil or grease.

- Small brush to loosen dirt and grime (a toothbrush is fine).

- Small screwdriver for prying shields (an eyeglasses screwdriver works well).

- Small tweezers to help with removing shields (optional).

Removing a Sealed Bearing

1. Remove one of the shields—not both.

2. Carefully insert the end of a small screwdriver between the shield and the inner race.

3. Pry shield up.

4. Continue to rotate and pry until the shield comes off.

5. At this point, a pair of tweezers will help you grip the shield. Using a twisting-pulling motion, remove the shield.

6. Now see "Technique."

Step 5

Technique (Unsealed Bearings)

1. Remove wheels from skates.

2. Remove bearings from wheel using a ⁵⁄₁₆-inch bolt from a hardware store, or similar-size tool, by pressing against the thin outer edge of the bearing spacer. (*Do not* press against bearing itself.)

3. Remove other bearing by hand.

Step 13

4. Lift rubber seal by inserting the tip of a straightened paper clip, or a small screwdriver, and prying upward.

5. With small screwdriver, push the retainer out of the opposite side of the bearing.

6. Place bearings, retainers, and seals in container with solvent, and soak (bath 1).

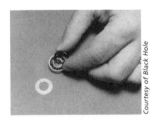

Step 14

7. Use parts brush for stubborn dirt and grime.

8. Spin bearing with fingers.

9. Place on rag/paper towels to drain.

10. Place bearings, retainers, and seals in second, clean solvent bath (bath 2).

11. Place on rag/paper towels to drain, and dry thoroughly.

12. When dry, place bearing on side.

Step 15

13. Position ball bearings with small screwdriver so there is equal space between each of them.

14. Position retainer on top of ball bearings and press firmly in place.

15. Select lubricating formula. Apply a drop or two—that's all.

16. On opposite side of bearing, place rubber seal back into place.

Step 16

It makes no difference in in-line roller hockey whether you use black or white tape. Ice hockey players tend to use black tape exclusively, because black tape makes it more difficult for the goaltender to see the black puck.

17. Spin bearing to distribute lubricant.

18. Place bearing back into wheel core.

Taping the Stick

The stick's shaft, blade, and knob should be taped.

Begin with spiral wraps, twisting the tape as you move down. This creates vertical ridges, making it easier to grip.

With a new piece of tape, start from the top of the stick and apply the tape flat (not twisted) over the ridges you created in the first step.

Some believe that taping the blade for in-line roller hockey is unnecessary, since the plastic puck is not as hard as its vulcanized rubber counterpart in ice hockey. Taping the blade is a matter of personal preference.

The Shaft

The stick's shaft should be taped to provide a better grip.

To properly tape the shaft, wrap one continuous strand of tape around it in the following manner: Twirl the tape around the top portion of the shaft (like a barber pole) to create vertical ridges. Next, tape over the ridges, this time applying the full width of the tape—do not twist it. Tear and press the tape down to shape it.

Wrap with tape from the toe of the blade to the heel.

The Blade

There are several advantages to taping your stick's blade.

1. Helps keep the puck from rolling off the end (or toe).

2. Helps prevent breaking, wearing, and cracking.

3. Helps cushion puck when receiving a pass.

When complete, your taped blade should look like this.

There is a tendency to apply more tape than is necessary. There is no point carrying around any more weight than you have to. Use the amount of tape that will benefit your play—no more and no less. Your coach or instructor can help.

Rubber knob covers can be used instead of tape. These are available at most stores that sell in-line roller hockey gear.

4. Helps to determine wear pattern, which indicates if your stick and lie are the proper size.

The Knob

The stick's knob (or "butt end") is taped so the stick does not slip out of your hand. This is especially helpful when you are holding the stick with one hand—when skating backward, for instance.

The knob should be comfortable and grippable. The ideal size and shape vary from player to player.

Storing Equipment and Supplies

Each player should have a hockey equipment bag. Whether your bag is team-provided or your own, it should be quite large, be water-repellent, and have plenty of ventilation holes.

Each team should establish and maintain an in-line roller hockey supply kit. This kit should be kept in a large athletic bag or duffel—or in a rigid chest or footlocker, most of which have the benefit of a lock and protect the contents from being crushed. Your team bag or chest can be decorated with your team logo and colors. It should contain both game supplies and a well-stocked first-aid kit.

Team Game Supplies

- A supply of pucks to be used for game warm-up or during practices. (About two or three new game pucks. Generally, the home team is required to provide these.)

- Extra blank jerseys in case anyone forgets his or one is damaged during play.

- Filled water bottles. Bottles with directional spouts are ideal, since they permit you to shoot a stream of water into the mouth without removing your helmet or cage. (About half a dozen.)

- White hand towels. Laundering can be assigned to players on a rotating basis. (About a dozen.)

- White hockey tape for taping knobs, shafts, and blades of hockey sticks. (About a dozen rolls.)

- Tape in team colors for various purposes—putting a number on a spare jersey or taping rosters on the wall, for example. (Three or four rolls.)

- Lockbox for holding players' keys and other valuables.

- Needle and thread for a variety of uses.

- Extra skate laces, equipment laces/straps, new mouthpieces, buckles, suspenders, etc.

Team First-Aid Kit

 If you cannot treat a medical problem with this well-equipped first-aid kit, then you should call in an Emergency Medical Services (EMS) team at once.

- Medical adhesive tape

- Sterile gauze pads

- Ace bandages

- Sling

- Band-Aids in assorted sizes

- Aspirin

- Disposable rubber gloves

- Foam rubber or moleskin in assorted sizes (for blisters, etc.)

- Tweezers

- Disinfectant

- Plastic bags for ice or cold packs

- Heat bags

- Ammonia inhalant (for fainting spells)

- Coins for pay telephone

- Complete medical history forms for each player, in the event of serious medical injury

- Medical emergency contact card

- Scissors/knife

- Disinfectant soap

- Mouth-opening appliance

- Safety pins

- CPR instruction sheet

Purchasing Equipment

Shopping Versus Buying

Everyone loves new things—especially when they are for a game as fun and exciting as in-line roller hockey. Whether you are buying a pair of in-line skates or a new suit, ultimately there are two ways you can approach the purchase. You can *buy* or you can *shop*. What's the difference? Plenty!

Buyers are an impulsive lot. Of course, we are all guilty of spending our money on something that we only later realize we will never use. (Look around your room. Do you see any unread books, unworn clothes, or long-abandoned compact discs?) Buyers are impatient and tend to buy the first item they see that appeals to them—whether it is appropriate for their needs or not.

Shoppers, on the other hand, consider a new purchase with forethought and care. They often start with a list of the items they need, set limits to what they can spend, and begin their investigation. Whether it is making a series of phone calls to seek the advice of trusted friends, or reading this book, a shopper knows that a well-considered "game plan" is the best way to purchase in-line roller hockey equipment. When a retailer starts reeling your mind by telling you he has a "special deal" on some skate wheels, do you know enough to ask an informed question? Do you know the importance of a wheel's profile and durometer?

One thing you can do to become informed is study the marketplace. Read product reviews and in-line skating and in-line roller hockey magazines. (See Appendix D for a listing.) If you have a computer, log on to Internet or a commercial on-line service and ask your questions. You will find many experts willing to help while cruising the net.

Knowing the language when traveling through the product maze of in-line roller hockey equipment is tantamount to speaking a little French when traveling in Paris. Whether you are in a Parisian taxicab or a Manhattan shop that sells in-line hockey gear, knowing the language will help you avoid being taken for a ride.

Where to Shop

As recently as 10 years ago, you would be hard-pressed to find in-line skates, let alone equipment specifically designed for in-line roller hockey. Times have changed.

 Get a specific recommendation from a friend. Mention that to the retailer when you come in—it is a great way to "break the ice," so to speak.

Today, one can find in-line skating and roller hockey equipment just about anywhere—department stores, toy stores, drugstores, camping and sporting goods stores, and elsewhere. But if you are a shopper, your initial concern in the purchasing process is *information*, and so you ask yourself, "What retailer is going to give me the most objective and factual information?"

Specialty In-line Skating/Roller Hockey Retailers

Speciality retailers are your best starting place. The retailer who specializes in in-line skating and in-line roller hockey equipment is a godsend for the in-line roller hockey player. First of all, this retailer is dedicated to the sport and is probably skating or playing in-line roller hockey as often as possible. Second, many in-line retailers treat you as a member of a special community—that is, with respect and patience. Now, do not be fooled, this is not pure altruism here. The retailer knows that a well-served customer is going to keep coming back and spending more money.

Sporting Goods Stores

General sporting-goods stores should be the second choice on your list of places to shop. Although they carry a variety of athletic equipment, you will probably be able to find someone knowledgeable about in-line roller hockey, or at least in-line skating. It always helps when your salesperson plays the game. There is nothing like real-life experience *and* product knowledge.

Used-Equipment Stores

Short on cash? Today there are more and more options for getting used, or "remanufactured," in-line roller hockey equipment. In fact, there is a specialty chain, Play It Again Sports, that is in the business of buying and selling used athletic equipment—including in-line roller hockey gear.

However, purchasing used equipment makes knowing about the equipment before you enter the store even more important. You need the kind of information that will allow you to identify specific components of a given piece of equipment so you can accurately assess its condition for yourself. If you are new to the game of in-line roller hockey, bring along a friend or teammate who can help you assess the condition of the equipment before you buy it.

You should also inquire about the availability of a product warranty. If the original manufacturer's warranty has expired, does the shop have any kind of shopper assurance plan? Do not be afraid to ask questions.

Shopping Checklist for Skates

Following is a list of items that you should consider when selecting in-line roller hockey equipment:

- Test boot for ankle support. Pinch boot at the upper-ankle area and bend from side to side. Too much flex? It may not offer enough ankle support.

- Is the frame sturdy? While sitting, hold the skate between the knees with wheels pointing up. Grip frame at opposite end and try twisting it. Is it strong and rigid?

- Check bearings. Are they good quality? Will you have to replace them immediately after you purchase your skates?

- Do the wheels suit your skating preference and playing surface? Note the ABEC rating and diameter when examining wheels.

- Wear socks like those you will be skating in when you try on skates for fit.

CHAPTER 3

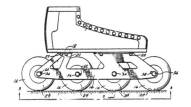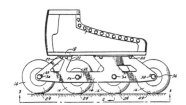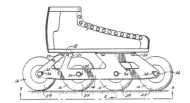

THE RULES

The following rules and regulations are excerpted from the *NIHA Official Rulebook*, which is derived, in part, from *Rules of the Game* (1958, The Diagram Group). Further modifications have been made based on the input and assistance of existing in-line roller hockey leagues, the International In-line Skating Association (IISA), and in-line manufacturers. These rules are officially recognized by the United States Amateur Confederation of Roller Skating (USAC/RS), the national governing body of all roller sports.

The Rink

The game of in-line roller hockey shall be played on a surface known as a rink. The rink can be outdoors and unprotected from the natural elements, outdoors and partially closed, or a fully enclosed indoor facility.

In large, vacant parking lots, a rink size of 200 feet by 100 feet is often available. This is safer than a smaller rink, because it allows for a larger area around the back of the goal. A player on in-line skates needs this area, because his skates do not permit him to turn as sharply as an ice hockey player.

Dimensions of Rink

As nearly as possible, the dimensions of the rink shall be 180 feet long by 80 feet wide. The rules allow surfaces ranging from as large as 200 feet by 100 feet wide to 145 feet long by 65 feet wide. Tournament or championship games must be played on rinks that are close to the ideal or official rink dimensions.

The rink must be surrounded by bordering material, known as the "structure," which will extend no less than 8 inches and not more than 48 inches above the playing surface.

The traditional size of an outdoor rink is 180 feet by 80 feet. The main reason for this is the size limitations of some of the primary sites for in-line roller hockey, like open or abandoned tennis and basketball courts, which are smaller than a standard hockey arena.

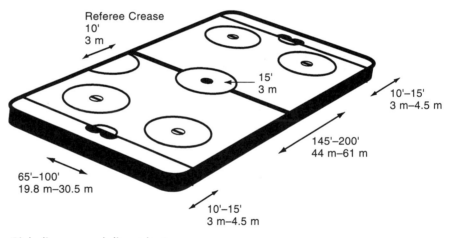

Rink diagram and dimensions

Division of the Rink Surface

The rink shall be divided into two halves, with a center line 12 inches wide. The center area (zone) of the rink is considered neither an attacking nor a defending area.

A team's goal area shall be called the "defending zone." The opposing team's area shall be known as the "attacking zone."

Center of Rink

A circular spot (preferably blue), 2 feet in diameter and placed on the center line, shall be the center of the rink. This will be the location where face-offs occur at the beginning of each period and after each goal.

Face-Off Spots

In each half of the two zones, there shall be two spots 2 feet in diameter of equal distance from the rink's side structure. Face-offs shall occur at these spots.

Goalposts and Nets

The official size of the goal is 72 inches between goalposts and 48 inches from the playing surface to the top of the net. These dimensions will be official for tournament and championship play. Alternative sizes are acceptable for regular league play.

A net must be attached to each goal frame. Each net must have goalposts and a crossbar.

Painted from post to post must be a line 2 inches wide. This is known as the "goal line." This line should be extended the width of the rink to assist the official in making a "clearing" call. The recommended area behind each goal net, measured from the goal line to the bordering structure, shall be 10 to 15 feet.

Goal Crease and Goalkeeper's Privileged Area

In front of each goal, a "goal crease" area shall be marked. The goal crease shall be a semicircle 6 feet in radius and 2 inches in width and shall be drawn using the center of the goal line as the center point.

The goalkeeper's privileged area shall extend 12 feet from the mouth of the goal and 12 feet on either side of the center of the goal. This

288-square-foot imaginary area allows a goalkeeper an extended playing zone. Stoppage of play by the goalkeeper outside of this area will be penalized.

Other Areas

Players' Bench

An area outside of the playing area shall be designated as the players' bench. Each rink shall have adequate space to accommodate two separate team benches.

Penalty Bench

Each rink shall provide a designated area outside the playing surface where a player(s) may serve penalty time. If possible, the penalty bench should be located on the opposite side of the playing surface from the players' bench.

Minor Officials' Bench and Referees' Crease

Each rink shall be equipped with an official clock and/or a designated timekeeper to monitor game and penalty time. This person (minor official) shall have a designated area (minor officials' bench) in which to sit. The referees' crease shall be marked by a 2-inch-wide line drawn in a semicircle at a radius of 10 feet from the minor officials' bench.

Equipment

Sticks

Sticks shall be made of materials approved by the NIHA Rules Committee and must not have any alterations. No stick shall exceed 62 inches in length from the heel to the end of the shaft, and no stick shall be more than 12 inches from the heel to the end of the blade. The blade shall be no more than 3.25 inches in width at any point, nor less than 1.75 inches at any point. All edges must be beveled.

Knob (Butt End)

Shaft

Blade   Lie

Toe   Heel

The curvature of the blade shall be restricted to the distance such that a perpendicular line measured from the base of the toe to the point of maximum curvature shall not exceed ¾ of an inch.

The blade of the goalkeeper's stick, extending the length of the shaft, shall not exceed 26 inches from the heel or exceed 3.5 inches in width. The wide portion of the goalkeeper's stick shall not exceed 26 inches from the heel or 3.5 inches in width.

A minor penalty shall be assessed to any player or goalkeeper who uses a stick in a way that does not conform to the provisions of this rule. The stick shall be removed from play in such a case. A minor penalty plus a game misconduct shall be assessed to any player who deliberately breaks a stick or refuses to surrender a stick to an official. The referee will take the stick to the referee crease to make the appropriate measurement.

Skates

Any skate not approved by the Rules Committee is prohibited. All players and referees must wear skates without modification. Brakes are optional.

Eye protection is strongly recommended.

 If a player is injured while not wearing any piece of the equipment listed here, the insurance carrier may not be responsible for the claim.

Protective Equipment

All players under the age of 18 are required to wear:

- Head protection (hockey helmet) with chin strap
- Face protection (full face mask or full face shield)
- Mouth guard—in mouth
- Elbow pads
- Hand protection (hockey gloves)
- Knee and shin protection
- Athletic supporter and protective cup (for boys)

All players 18 years and older (adult) are required to wear:

- Head protection (hockey helmet) with chin strap
- Mouth guard—in mouth
- Elbow pads
- Hand protection (hockey gloves)
- Knee and shin protection
- Athletic supporter and protective cup (for males)

The equipment listed here shall be mandatory for all youth players who have been approved for excess medical coverage from NIHA. Any default shall be at the player's and/or guardian's risk.

A player, excluding the goalkeeper, whose helmet or face mask falls off during play must immediately go to his bench and may not resume play until the helmet or mask has been properly refitted. Failure to do so will result in a penalty.

Goalkeeper's Equipment

With the exception of skates and the stick, all equipment worn by the goalkeeper must be constructed solely for the purpose of protecting the head or body, and he may not wear any garment or use any aid that would give him an unfair advantage in keeping goal.

The individual leg pads worn by the goalkeeper shall not exceed 12 inches in extreme width when fastened to the leg. The goalkeeper's

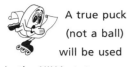

A true puck (not a ball) will be used in the NIHA state, regional, and national playoffs.

blocker shall not exceed 8 inches in width or 16 inches in length. The goalkeeper's catch glove shall not exceed 9 inches in width, including any attachments to the glove. The length of the catch glove shall not exceed 16 inches.

It is mandatory for all goalkeepers to wear helmets and full face masks. If a goalkeeper's helmet or face mask falls off during play, the referee shall stop play immediately. A minor penalty shall be given to a goalkeeper who deliberately removes his mask or helmet during play.

A minor penalty shall be assessed to a goalkeeper using illegal equipment in the game.

Dangerous Equipment

Use of pads or protectors made of metal or any other material that may cause harm to another player is prohibited and may result in a misconduct penalty. A glove from which all or part of the palm and/or fingers has been cut or worn away to allow the bare hand or fingers to be exposed shall be considered illegal equipment. A minor penalty shall be assessed to any player wearing such equipment.

Puck

The puck shall be made of any material approved by the National Inline Hockey Association. The puck shall be one color and contrast with the playing surface.

The Game

The game is played on a reasonably flat surface free of debris and obstacles. The surface may be indoors or outdoors. The game is played between two teams of four skaters and one goalie. The object of the game is to advance the puck down the rink past the opponents' goalkeeper and into the net. The team with the most goals at the end of the allotted time period is declared the winner.

No intentional body contact is allowed. Accidental or incidental contact is permitted. It shall be left to the officials' discretion to determine if any body contact between two players warrants a penalty.

Time of Match

A 1-hour time frame is prescribed, since most indoor roller rink owners charge on an hourly basis. Regardless of the cost, 1 hour should provide a more-than-adequate workout, especially considering the fast and furious pace of the game.

The maximum time allotted for a game is 1 hour from the time a team enters the rink to the conclusion of the match. The match shall be made up of two equal halves.

The following options are allowed:

- A 5-minute warm-up period before the start of the game.
- Two 22-minute running-time halves with a 5-minute rest period between halves. Running time is recommended when there is no visible game clock.
- Two 12- to 15-minute stop-time halves with a 5-minute rest period between halves.

Each team will be allowed a 1-minute time-out to be used during regulation time only.

Weather Delays

Play will be stopped immediately in the event of rain or any other condition that may create moisture on the playing surface.

Is your league ready for the big time? An electronic scoreboard with a stop clock and player-penalty panel makes playing a game in stop-time format possible. Perhaps with a local sponsor's help and advertising space, your league can afford the big time too.

The game will resume at the exact game time play was interrupted, provided the surface is dry. If the conditions persist and the game does not resume within 30 minutes from the initial stoppage, and there is more than 5 minutes of playing time remaining, the game will be canceled and rescheduled by the league manager.

In the event that there is less than 5 minutes of playing time remaining at the time of cancellation, the team with the most goals will be declared the winner.

Choice of Goals

The home team shall select which goal they will defend at the start of a game. If there is no designated home team, the decision will be determined by the toss of a coin, with the captains from each team participating in the coin toss.

Beginning Play

The game begins with a face-off at the center rink face-off spot; this is repeated at the start of the second half of play. The puck is faced off when the referee drops the puck on the rink between the sticks of the players facing off. Players facing off must stand squarely facing each other's end of the rink, approximately one stick length apart with the blades of their sticks touching the surface of the rink. No other players may come within a 10-foot radius of players facing off and all players must be "on side" during all face-offs.

During a face-off, no player may begin play until the puck is dropped. If a player does not leave the face-off area after being directed to do so by an official, the player may be assessed a minor penalty.

Puck Must Be Kept in Motion

Except to carry the puck behind the net, a team in possession of the puck in its own (defending) zone must always advance play with the intention of scoring on the opposing goal, except if prevented from doing so by players on the opposing team.

A minor penalty shall be assessed to any player or goalkeeper who holds the puck with his stick, skates, or body along the rink walls in such a manner as to cause stoppage of play, unless he is being pursued by an opponent.

Puck Out of Bounds or Frozen

It is recommended that the minor officials' bench always keep an extra puck.

When the puck goes outside the playing area, it shall be considered "out of play" and faced off at the nearest face-off spot, or a point equidistant from the boundary structure and the point at which it left the playing surface.

When a puck becomes lodged in the goal netting and is unplayable, or if it is "frozen" between opposing players, unintentionally or otherwise, the official shall blow the whistle to signal a face-off at the nearest face-off spot. A minor penalty shall be assessed against a goalkeeper who deliberately drops the puck on the goal netting to cause a stoppage of play.

Puck Out of Sight

If the puck goes out of sight of the game officials, the referee shall blow the whistle to signal stoppage of play. Play shall resume with a face-off at the nearest face-off spot.

Puck Striking Official

Play shall not stop if the puck strikes the official anywhere within the rink during play.

Goals and Assists

It is the responsibility of the referee to award goals and assists. Such calls shall be considered final.

A goal shall be scored when the puck has completely crossed the goal line.

A goal shall be scored if a player from the defending team puts or deflects the puck into his own net in any way. In such a case, the last player to touch the puck from the attacking team shall be awarded the goal, but no assist will be recorded.

A goal can be scored off a player's stick only if the puck is contacted by the stick below the waist.

A goal shall be scored from a deflection of an attacking player, including his skate, provided the player is outside the goal crease. A goal shall also be scored if the attacking player has been involuntarily moved into the opposing goalkeeper's crease by a defending player.

If an attacking player kicks the puck directly into the net, or if the kicked puck deflects off another player and/or goalkeeper, a goal shall not be awarded.

If a puck that has been deflected off an official goes into the net, a goal shall not be awarded.

When a goal is scored, an assist shall be awarded to the player who passes the puck to the player who scores the goal. No more than one assist may be awarded per goal scored. Each goal and assist recorded shall count as a point on the player's record.

Tied Game

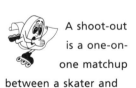

A shoot-out is a one-on-one matchup between a skater and the opposing goal-keeper. A player takes the puck from the center face-off spot and attempts to score a goal. The goalkeeper may not move from the goalkeeper's crease until the puck is touched by the opposing player.

If the score is tied at the end of regulation play, each team shall be awarded one point in league standing. There shall be no overtime play during the regular season. In tournament or league playoffs, there will be a five-minute overtime period to decide games that are tied after regulation time has expired. All normal rules apply during this period.

If the score remains tied after the overtime period, a "shoot-out" overtime will commence, with four players on each team allowed one opportunity to score. The team with the most goals scored during the "shoot-out" shall be declared the winner.

The five-minute overtime period is considered a continuation of the game, and any unexpired penalties shall remain in effect.

 Often it is the action and move- ment of the attacking player that causes interference, since the defending players are allowed to stand ground.

Occasionally players of marginal skating ability may create the appearance of interference. An official should call a penalty only for the three types of delib- erate interference:

1. Deliberately impeding the movement of an opposing player after the puck has been faced off.

2. Deliberately holding the stick of an opposing player.

3. Making a drop pass and following through so as to take an opponent out of play, thus opening the way for the puck carrier.

Point System

The winning team shall receive two points in the league standings. The losing team shall receive no points. In the event of a tied game, each team shall receive one point each.

Adjustment of Clothing and Equipment

A player shall not be permitted to request stoppage of time to adjust clothing or equipment. If adjustments are necessary, the player shall return to the player's bench and another player shall enter the game. The goalkeeper may receive time to adjust padding without being substituted, but only following a stoppage of play.

Broken Stick

A player or goalkeeper whose stick has been broken must drop the stick immediately. A minor penalty shall be assessed for an infraction of this rule. If his team throws him a replacement stick, he shall receive a penalty. A replacement stick may be passed only from hand to hand.

Interference

It is a violation of the rules to interfere with or otherwise impede the progress of any opponent who is not in possession of the puck. Accidental or incidental body contact will be permitted, however. All judgments in this case shall be at the referees' discretion.

Kicking the Puck

Kicking the puck with a skate shall be permitted in all zones. However, a puck kicked into the goal or deflected off a player, including the goalkeeper, shall not be counted as a goal.

 If an NIHA league wishes to use a center-line offside rule, it may use the modified offside rule:

1. The player with the puck must have full control as he crosses the center line.

2. If an attacking player precedes the puck, which is shot, passed, or deflected into the attacking zone, but a defending player is able to play the puck, then the referee shall allow play to continue and no offside penalty shall be called. (A) The defending team must pass or carry the puck. (B) All attacking players must clear the offensive zone by leaving it or making skate contact with the center line.

3. The attacking team may have player(s) other than the player with the puck in the attacking zone. However, these other players may not touch the puck until after the player with the puck enters the attacking zone in control of the puck.

In the Goal Crease

A goal will be disallowed if an attacking player is in the goal crease area before the puck enters the net. If the player is pushed into the goal crease by a member of the defending team, the goal will be allowed.

An attacking player who has possession of the puck may enter the goal crease while attempting to score.

Player Altercation

No player may leave the players' bench or penalty box to participate in an on-surface altercation. Any violation of this rule will result in a gross misconduct penalty.

Center Line Offside

There will be no official center-line offside penalty in in-line roller hockey.

Clearing

The puck may not be shot or passed from the defensive zone to the opposite end of the rink and across the goal line, without having the puck touched by a player. There will be a stoppage in play and a face-off in the defensive zone of the team that shoots or passes the puck in this manner.

The Team

Composition

A team shall be composed of four skaters and a goalkeeper. (A total of five players on the playing surface.) A maximum of 12 players, including goalkeepers, will be allowed on any single team roster. No

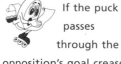

If the puck passes through the opposition's goal crease, the clearing infraction will be nullified.

player may be on two different rosters in the same league, with the exception of goalkeepers.

Team Captain

One captain shall be appointed by each team. Only he shall have the privilege of conferring with the referee on the playing surface. The captain should wear the letter C on the front, upper left-hand corner of his jersey; the letter should be approximately 3.5 inches in height and contrast in color with the jersey.

If the team captain is not available because of injury or penalty, the first assistant shall act as "designated" captain. The assistant shall be noted in the player roster.

Player Roster

At the beginning of the season, the captain of each team will submit to the league or club manager a roster of players who are eligible for play. Any additions to this roster must be made prior to the midseason point on the schedule. No additions will be permitted after this point.

A list of the names and numbers of eligible players must be submitted to the referee or official before each game. This roster may not be changed once the game has commenced.

Players listed on the player roster must wear the same-color jerseys. Numbers at least 8 inches in height must be affixed to the back of the player jerseys. For state, regional, and national play-offs, a backup goalkeeper must be designated in the event of an injury or illness.

Player Substitution

A goalkeeper may reenter the game only at a stoppage of play.

Players may be substituted at any time from the players' bench. Exiting players must not interfere with play while leaving the playing surface. The exchange may be made only within 10 feet of the players' bench. A "too many player" penalty shall be called if an exiting player attempts to "play" the puck while leaving the surface. A goalkeeper may be replaced at any time by a skater. The goalkeeper must be within 10 feet of the players' bench before the substitute player may step onto the playing surface.

Any player who, while not on the playing surface, deliberately attempts to obstruct play by throwing debris, or reaches for the puck or a player, shall be assessed a minor penalty. If a puck is headed for an empty net while the goalkeeper is off the playing surface and a player on the bench attempts to interfere, a goal will be scored for the opposing team.

Injured Players

If a player is injured, he will remove himself from the rink without the assistance of another player. He shall do so without a stoppage of play. An official may warn a player who appears to be using time to delay play. This rule also applies to goalkeepers. If an injured player cannot remove himself, play will stop and time will be called so as to remove the injured player from the surface.

An injured penalized player may go straight to the locker room and another player may serve the penalty.

Penalties

Minor Penalties

For a minor penalty the offending player shall be removed from play for two minutes (running time) from the time the puck is dropped to restart play. His team will play with one less player.

For a bench minor penalty (an infraction by the team, not an individual player), the captain or coach of the offending team will assign a player (either on or off the playing surface) to serve two minutes. His team will play short one player.

If the opposing team scores a goal while a team is shorthanded, the shorthanded team shall be permitted to immediately regain the first player who caused his team to be shorthanded.

Major Penalties

In cases where two minor penalties have been assessed to the same team, the penalty time of the second player that enters the penalty box does not commence until the first player's penalty has expired or a goal has been scored against his team.

For the first major penalty assessed to a player in any single game, he shall be removed from the playing surface for 5 minutes. (For the goalkeeper there are special rules; see "Goalkeeper Penalties.") For a second major penalty assessed to a player in a single game, a game misconduct penalty, in addition to a major penalty, will be given. The player will also be suspended from playing the remainder of the game.

If a player receives a major and minor penalty, the major penalty shall be served first. When two players on the same team receive penalties, one minor and one major, the minor penalty shall be served first.

Minor and major penalties shall be imposed for the following infractions (the severity of the penalty shall be left to the referee's discretion):

Poor Conduct

- Challenging or disputing the decision of the referee
- Creating a disturbance
- Shooting the puck after the whistle has blown
- Delaying the game by deliberately throwing or shooting the puck out of the playing area
- Deliberately displacing the goal net
- Using obscene or abusive language
- Interfering in any way with a game official
- Interference of play from the bench
- Making physical contact with an opponent after the whistle has blown
- Abuse of officials (verbal or physical)
- Failure to heed the decisions of an official after a penalty has been called
- Throwing anything into the playing area

Excessive Violence

- Deliberate bodychecking
- Running, jumping, kicking, or charging an opponent
- Cross-checking
- Unnecessary roughness
- Use of forearms or hands to check an opponent above the opponent's shoulder

Injury or Attempt to Injure

- Slashing or attempts to slash
- Butt-ending or attempts to butt-end

Altercation (Fighting, Wrestling)

- Physical retaliation against an opposing player

Obstructions

- Elbowing or kneeing
- Holding an opponent or his stick in a manner that impedes him from playing
- Tripping
- Defending player (excluding the goalkeeper) smothering the puck
- Goalkeeper smothering the puck outside the privileged area
- Impeding the progress of an opponent who does not have control of the puck, knocking his stick from the hands, or preventing him from retrieving it

Technical Violation

- Use of a stick not conforming to the rules
- Leaving the penalty box prior to expiration of the penalty
- Throwing a stick in the direction of the puck

Delaying the Game

- Failure to maintain proper face-off position
- Deliberately holding the puck against the surface structure
- Exceeding the maximum number of players in play
- Excessive clearing (referee's discretion)

 Wild swinging at an opponent or at the puck to intimidate an opponent is considered an infraction warranting a major penalty.

The following infractions always result in a major penalty:

- Injuring an opponent by cross-checking or hooking
- Injuring an opponent by deliberate use of the knee or elbow
- Grabbing or holding the face mask of an opponent
- Injuring an opponent by slashing
- Deliberate intent to injure an opponent

Zero Tolerance Rule

 This rule is very strictly enforced. In-line roller hockey under NIHA rules is intended for the whole family. Although we all lose our tempers from time to time, you have to learn that "venting" with a string of four-letter words is not appropriate.

If any official hears either a player on the skating surface or a team member on the bench use profane language, a 2-minute bench penalty will be assessed, an on-surface player will serve the penalty, and the team will play one player short for the duration of the penalty.

If the offending language continues, the referee may default the game and award the points to the opposing team.

Misconduct Penalties

A *misconduct penalty* calls for the removal of a player other than the goalkeeper from the game for a period of 10 minutes. However, another player is permitted to replace the removed player. After the penalty has expired, the player may not return to the game until there is a stoppage in play. A player assessed a misconduct along with another penalty will serve both penalties consecutively (back-to-back).

A *game misconduct* penalty involves the suspension of a player or team official for the remainder of the game; a player also will have to sit out the next league or playoff game. A team may replace the

 Any player or team official who is assessed a game misconduct penalty shall automatically be suspended for a minimum of the next league or playoff game. (Ten minutes will be charged in the records against the penalized player.)

penalized player with a substitute. A game misconduct penalty may be assessed if what is normally a minor infraction causes an opponent to bleed.

A *gross misconduct* penalty calls for the suspension of a player for the remainder of the game. A team may replace the suspended player with a substitute. The player or team official, however, will not be allowed to participate in other games until the case has been reviewed by the league manager or the NIHA Disciplinary Committee.

The following infractions result in a major penalty:

Abuse of Officials

1. An aggressive dispute by a player with an official after a penalty has been called

2. Using obscene or abusive language

3. Intentionally shooting or knocking the puck onto the playing surface

4. Deliberately throwing the puck or equipment onto the playing surface

5. Entering the referee's crease while the referee is consulting with off-surface officials

6. Touching or holding a game official in any way

7. Spearing, attempting to spear, or making a spearing gesture at a player

8. Fighting (an automatic game misconduct)

9. Any behavior that the referee views as detrimental to the game

Match Penalties

A *match penalty* is the suspension of a player for the remainder of the game. The suspended player must return to the locker room or otherwise leave the rink area. A team may replace the player after a 5-minute penalty has been served.

Suspension Penalties

Suspension penalties will be assessed for the following match penalties:

1. Deliberate attempt to injure a player. This includes fighting, slashing, spearing, intentional tripping, etc. A referee may invoke a match penalty and remove a player who is intentionally causing harm to other players.

2. Kicking a player. A referee may impose an automatic suspension, subject to further review by the league manager.

Penalty Shot

A penalty shot may be awarded to a team for any of the following reasons:

1. A player (other than the goalkeeper) deliberately gathers the puck in the crease and smothers it.

2. An attacking player has a "breakaway" (no one between the attacking player and the defending goalkeeper) and is illegally prevented by the defending team from advancing toward the goalkeeper.

3. Throwing a stick or any other object at the puck in the defending zone while the attacking team is attempting to score. If this is done on an open net (the goalie has been removed), a goal will be awarded.

Penalty-Shot Execution

For a penalty shot the referee will place the puck at the center-rink face-off spot. The referee will then signal play to begin. The player must maintain a forward motion at all times. No goal may be scored from a rebound. The goalkeeper must remain in the crease until the shooting player has made contact with the puck. If the goalkeeper leaves the crease prematurely, the referee will start the play again.

During a penalty shot, all other players must return to their respective benches. If a goal is scored, there will be a center-rink face-off. If no goal is scored, a face-off will occur in the defending team's zone.

Goalkeeper Penalties

A goalkeeper shall not be removed from the net for a minor or major penalty. Instead, another team member will serve the goalkeeper's penalty. A goalkeeper who receives a game or match misconduct will be removed from the game and replaced by a substitute goalkeeper. This player will be granted a reasonable amount of time to put on the goalkeeper equipment and limber up.

A goalkeeper may be suspended for future games if the infraction is deemed serious by the league manager. A minor penalty shall be assessed to a goalkeeper who leaves the goal crease during a fight or who engages in play beyond the center line.

Calling of Penalties

An infraction of the rules by a team with possession of the puck shall be called immediately, and the referee will stop play. If the offending team is not in possession of the puck at the moment of the infraction, the referee shall raise his arm and play will continue until the offending team touches the puck. (This is called a "delayed penalty.") Then the referee shall stop play and call the penalty. Until play has stopped, the attacking team may replace their goalkeeper with another offensive player.

The subsequent face-off shall be where the infraction took place. Following a delayed call, the face-off will take place in the offending team's zone, inside the center line.

Referees

The referees shall maintain control of the game and the players. Any decision made by a referee is final. The referee has control over stoppage of play and the game clock. The referee shall assign an official timekeeper and scorekeeper at the beginning of each game.

The scorekeeper will also record penalties. Each game shall have a minimum of one referee and a maximum of two. Players who excessively argue a referee's decision(s) may be removed from the game and/or face suspension.

Holding: Clasp the wrist of the whistle hand with the other hand well in front of the chest.

Hooking: Make a series of tugging motions with both arms, as if pulling something toward the stomach.

Interference: Cross arms with the fists clenched in front of the chest.

Boarding: Strike the clenched fist of one hand into the open palm of the other hand directly in front of the chest.

Delayed calling of penalty: Point with an open palm, fingers together, one time with the free hand.

International offside: After sounding the whistle for offsides, point toward the offending team's special spot with the non-whistle hand.

Delay of game: The non-whistle hand, palm open, is placed across the chest and then fully extended directly in front of the body.

Goal scored: Point at the net with the non-whistle hand, palm open, and sound the whistle.

Roughing: Fully extend the arm in front of the body with a clenched fist. (Checking is considered a roughing penalty.)

Butt-ending: Make a crossing motion of the forearms, one moving under the other.

Charging: Rotate the clenched fists around one another in front of the chest.

Delayed or slow whistle: Raise free arm straight up. If play returns to the neutral zone without stoppage, draw the arm down the instant the puck/ball crosses the line (a penalty in a single-referee system).

High sticking: Hold both fists clenched to the side of the head, one a short distance immediately above the other.

Elbowing: Tap the elbow with the opposite hand.

Grasping the face mask: A single or double motion, as if grasping a face mask and pulling it downward.

Time out: Using both hands, form a "T" in front of the chest.

Hitting from behind: Arm is placed behind the back, elbow is bent, forearm is parallel to the surface.

Spearing: Make a single jabbing motion with both hands together, thrust forward in front of the chest, then drop the hands to the side.

Cross checking: Make a single forward-and-back motion with both fists clenched in front of the chest.

Slashing: Chop once with the non-whistle hand across the extended forearm of the other hand.

Misconduct: Hands should be moved once from the sides down to the hips. Thus, point to the player first and then bring the hands to the hips.

Penalty shot: Arms are crossed over head, and fists are clenched.

Kneeing: Slap the right palm to the right knee once. (Both skates remain on the surface.)

Tripping: Slap right hand on the right leg. Keep both skates on the surface.

Clearing: The back referee signals the clearing situation by fully extending the free arm (i.e., without whistle) over the head. The referee (or linesperson) indicates the clearing is completed by extending the free arm over the head and up straight while blowing the whistle.

Washout: Swing both arms out to shoulder height. (1) When used by the referee this signal means "no goal" and "no high-sticking the puck/ball." (2) When used by a linesperson, it means "no clearing" and/or "no high-sticking the puck/ball" only. (3) Used to indicate when a player deliberately falls to the surface to draw a penalty.

CHAPTER 4

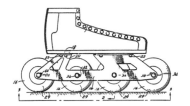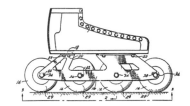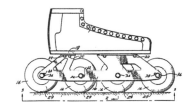

FOOT CARE AND FIRST AID

Safety Checklist

Before every game or practice, go through the following checklist:

- Axles and wheels are tight.

- Bearings do not need replacing.

- Wheel wear is not excessive. If it is, rotate the wheels.

- Protective gear is secure.

Seeing to these matters will greatly increase your chances of remaining injury-free. But you can be certain that at some point you will either sustain or witness some type of physical breakdown related to the unique nature of the sport. As you might expect, the most

77

common ailments of this sort are those affecting the feet. But foot ailments stemming from in-line roller hockey are also quite treatable.

Foot Care

Blisters

Blisters are pockets of fluid or blood beneath the outer layer of the skin. Constant irritation and rubbing of the boot and sock against the skin is most often the culprit. This is especially true if you are breaking in a new boot made of a tough material like leather. Most blisters go away by themselves once the cause is remedied, but occasionally they need to be drained. Infection is the major complication.

Treatment

1. Remove the source of irritation.

2. In general, blisters are better off left alone. The fluid inside will be gradually reabsorbed.

3. Keep the blister covered with a Band-Aid or gauze and tape.

4. If the blister breaks on its own, wash the area carefully with soap and water. Keep it covered, but observe daily for redness, drainage of pus, or swelling.

5. If the blister must be opened, clean it first with soap and water. Sterilize a needle by heating it over a flame until red hot. When the needle cools down, pierce the lower edge of the blister and allow fluid to escape. Use your finger to squeeze out the remainder. Cover with a clean bandage.

6. See your doctor if there are signs of infection, if the blister is large, or if it was caused by a burn, frostbite, or poison ivy.

Ingrown Toenail

Poor nail-trimming practices, tightly fitting shoes, and nail deformities may cause the corner of a toenail to grow into the adjoining skin.

The big toe is affected more than any other. The area soon becomes infected and very painful. Treatment usually involves at least partial removal of the nail.

Prevention

1. Keep your feet clean and dry.

2. Trim your toenails regularly. Cut straight across the ends so that the corners don't grow out. Not too short.

3. Wear socks.

4. Wear good-fitting shoes. Tight shoes push the toes together. Avoid high heels if you have this problem.

Treatment

 Persons with diabetes or circulatory problems can develop serious complications related to infection. They should be extra careful!

1. As soon as you notice nail pain, redness, and swelling, stay off your feet as much as possible. Prop up the affected foot on a cushion or footstool.

2. Soak in warm water or salt water for 10 to 15 minutes, three to four times each day.

3. After each soaking, insert a small piece of cotton gauze soaked in Betadine (antiseptic) beneath the corner of the nail. Cover with a light gauze. Tannic acid solutions (e.g., Outgro) may toughen the skin enough to allow you to cut the nail.

4. See your doctor for further therapy. Nail removal under local anesthesia and perhaps antibiotics will do the trick.

Athlete's Foot

Athlete's foot is a bothersome fungus infection of the toes and foot—think of it as ringworm of the feet. It is typically found between the fourth and fifth toes and is characterized by an itchy, scaly, odorous rash. Cracks, irritation, redness, and bacterial infections compound the problem.

Warm, moist conditions and skates that do not allow the feet to "breathe" are two contributing factors. Most susceptible are people who have previously had the infection, adult men, those whose feet perspire heavily, and those with weakened immunity to infection. Statistically, this is an adult man's problem more than any other group. Children, women, and those who go barefoot often do not have this problem.

It is widely believed that this fungus is acquired and spread in locker rooms and public bathrooms. In fact, this is often not the case. Surprisingly, in this age of medical miracles, the exact way in which athlete's foot is spread is not fully understood. We do know that it is caused by a fungus and that it develops best in warm and moist environments—like a sweating sock in a hockey boot!

Treatment

1. Mild cases can be treated at home without a visit to the doctor. The most important part of treatment is keeping the feet dry, especially the area between the toes.

2. Wear open-toed shoes or sandals when you have to have any footwear on at all. Avoid vinyl uppers and athletic shoes with rubber soles. Cotton socks are better than synthetics.

3. Wash your feet and soak them in a white vinegar/water solution (2–4 tablespoons/pint) for 20 minutes, two to three times a day.

4. Keep the toes wedged apart with gauze or cotton, and use foot powder to stay dry.

5. Many effective nonprescription medications may be found at your local pharmacy or grocery store. Follow the directions closely.

6. Be patient. It may take 2 weeks to 2 months for athlete's foot to clear up.

7. See your doctor if problems persist.

Athlete's foot in its early stages responds well to common antifungal powders and creams. To avoid athlete's foot in the future, make sure that you wash between the toes and dry them thoroughly before putting on a clean, dry pair of cotton socks.

First Aid

RICE

RICE is a mnemonic device (a memory aid) that will help you apply the basic steps in the care of minor injuries you may encounter while playing in-line roller hockey. It stands for the following:

R = Rest. Stop participating in your game or practice.

I = Ice. Apply ice or a cold compress to the injured area. Keep the ice on for 15 minutes, then remove for 20 minutes. Repeat this sequence several times. Icing should continue several times a day for the first three days following the injury.

C = Compression. Wrap a bandage around the injured area and the ice bag to hold it in place. Do not wrap the bandage so tight that it cuts off blood circulation to the injured area.

E = Elevation.

ABC

ABC is another mnemonic device to help you remember the sequence of steps to take when a player is not breathing or if his heart is not beating.

A = Airway. Clear the airway.

B = Breathing. Restore breathing.

C = Circulation. Restore blood circulation.

Treatment for Injury

Following are some specific situations requiring immediate treatment.

Injury   Dehydration

Cause   Lack of water in the body.

Symptoms Extreme thirst. Tiredness. Light-headedness. Abdominal or muscle cramps.

Treatment • Move player to shade.

• Replace lost fluids. Give player water or a commercial electrolyte-replacement fluid (e.g., Gatorade).

• Seek medical attention if symptoms persist.

Injury Back injury (lower back)

Causes Repetitive motion. Sudden force exerted on back. Insufficient warm-up period.

Symptoms From dull to sharp pain in lower back. If a muscle tears, slight pull may be felt when injury occurs. Herniated disc may produce sharp pain that makes movement impossible.

Treatment Tears and pulls:

• Place ice pack on back immediately. This will help alleviate swelling.

Stiffness and fatigue:

• Place heat pack on back. Lie down to ease pressure on back.

Injury Bruise

Cause Fall or blow to the body causes small blood vessels to break beneath the skin.

Symptoms Pain. Initial reddening of the skin. Later, bruise turns blue-green. Possible lump formation. Finally, area becomes brown-yellow before fading.

Treatment	• Apply cold pack to affected area to decrease internal bleeding/swelling.
	• If bruise is on arm/leg, elevate the limb above the heart.
	• After 24 hours, apply moist heat (warm wet compress).
	• If bruise is severe or painful, seek medical attention.
Injury	Knocked-out tooth
Cause	Puck, stick, etc. strikes mouth not protected by a face mask or cage.
Symptoms	Pain. Bleeding. Localized swelling.
Treatment	• Place ice pack on the affected area of the face.
	• If there is bleeding, fold clean piece of gauze, handkerchief, or tissue into a pad and place over wound. Close teeth and maintain pressure for 20 to 30 minutes at a time.
	• Wrap tooth in cool, wet cloth or place it in whole (not skim) milk. *Do not* put tooth in tap water. However, saline water may be used.
	• Take player to dentist or hospital emergency room immediately.
Injury	Bone dislocation
Cause	Fall or blow to the bone.
Symptoms	End of bone is displaced from joint. Swelling. Deformity at joint. Pain upon moving injured part or inability to

move. Discoloration of the skin around injury. Tenderness upon touching affected area.

Treatment
- *Do not* try to put dislocated bone back into place.

- Place player in comfortable position.

- Immobilize injured part with splint, pillow, or sling, in the position it was found.

- Seek medical attention promptly.

Injury   Eye injury (from hard, direct blow)

Cause   Hard, direct blow to eye from a puck, stick, etc.

Symptoms   Redness. Swelling. Pain. Possible internal bleeding in the eye.

Treatment
- Apply cold compress (ice wrapped in towel) to the injured eye.

- Keep player lying down with eyes closed if possible.

- Seek medical attention.

Injury   Eye injury (cuts)

Cause   Hard, direct blow to eye from a puck, stick, etc.

Symptoms   Redness. Swelling. Pain.

Treatment
- Cover injured eye with sterile pad or gauze or a clean, folded cloth, and bandage in place. *Do not* apply pressure. Also, cover uninjured eye to prevent eyeball movement.

- Seek medical attention immediately.

- Transport player lying down flat on back.

Drink up. Getting plenty of fluids before, during, and after the play is the best way to avoid dehydration or—worse—heat stroke.

Injury   Heat exhaustion

Cause   Prolonged exposure to high temperatures and high humidity.

Symptoms   Body temperature normal or slightly above normal. Pale and clammy skin. Heavy sweating. Tiredness, weakness, dizziness. Headache. Nausea. Possible muscle cramps, vomiting, or fainting.

Treatment   • Move player to shade or cooler area.

 • Have player lie down.

 • Raise player's feet 8 to 12 inches.

 • Loosen player's clothing.

 • If player is not vomiting, give clear juice or sips of cool salt water. Stop fluids if vomiting occurs.

 • Apply cool, wet cloths to player's forehead and body.

 • Use fan to cool the player. Or, if possible, move player to an air-conditioned room.

 • If symptoms are severe, become worse, or last more than an hour, seek medical attention.

Injury	Heatstroke (sunstroke) LIFE-THREATENING EMERGENCY
Causes	Exposure to heat and an inability of the body to cool itself.
Symptoms	Extremely high body temperature (often 106°F or higher). Red, hot, and dry skin. Sweating is usually absent. Rapid and strong pulse rate. Possible unconsciousness or confusion.
Treatment	If body reaches 105°F or greater:

- ABC procedure.

- Undress player and place in tub of cold water (not iced), if possible. Alternatively, spray player with water, sponge bare skin with cool water, or apply cold packs to player's body.

- Continue treatment until body temperature is lowered to 101°F or 102°F.

- Do not overchill. Check temperature constantly.

- Dry off player once temperature is lowered.

- Seek medical attention promptly.

Injury	Sprain
Cause	Overextending or twisting a limb beyond its normal range of movement.
Symptoms	Swelling of the joint. Tenderness upon touching the affected area. Discoloration of the skin around the area of the injury.
Treatment	If uncertain as to whether the injury is a sprain or a broken bone, treat as a broken bone.

 Our knees are arguably the most poorly designed joint we have. Consequently, they are often the first to break down on us, so we need to treat them with exceptional care. Always keep your knees warm (in cold), well protected, and flexible through stretching and warm-up routines. Finally, always be aware of internal "knee alerts"—pain under the kneecap and clicking and creaking sounds when bending. If you feel pain, tell your coach and stop playing.

For the ankle or knee:

- Place a small ice bag wrapped in a cloth over the affected area on and off for the first 12 to 24 hours.

- Apply supporting bandage. Loosen support if swelling increases.

- Keep injured area elevated above the level of the heart.

- Keep the player from walking if possible.

- *Do not* use heat or hot water soaks immediately following the injury. Wait at least 24 hours before applying heat.

- Seek medical attention in case there is a broken bone.

For the wrist or elbow:

- Place injured arm in a sling.

- Place cold wet packs or a small ice bag wrapped in cloth over the affected area. *Do not* apply heat for at least 24 hours after injury occurs.

- For wrist injury, apply a supporting bandage. Loosen bandage if swelling increases.

- Seek medical attention in case there is a broken bone.

Injury	Knee injury (torn ligament)
Cause	Sudden blow to the knee when the leg is straight.
Symptoms	Swelling and pain in the knee. Limited motion. Stiffness. Knee may go out of place.
Treatment	• Apply an ice pack to the knee.

- Avoid walking on the injured leg.

- See a physician for a proper diagnosis.

Injury   Muscle cramp

Cause   Usually, overuse during an extended game or practice.

Symptoms   Pain (often extreme). Stopping the activity can make the pain worse, but continuing activity is often impossible.

Treatment   • Direct massage.

- Apply heating pad on cramped muscle to help relieve tightness.

- Get player to hospital emergency room as soon as possible.

Injury   Shoulder separation

Causes   Blow or fall to the shoulder area. Falling on outstretched hand or arm.

Symptoms   Severe pain. Limited movement in the shoulder area. Swelling, bruising, internal bleeding.

Treatment   • Apply an ice pack.

- Seek medical treatment at once.

Injury   Head injury

Cause   A fall or a blow to the head, or a collision with an object or another player.

Any or all movement of the head, either forward, backward, or from side to side, can result in paralysis or death. However, if player must be moved due to imminent danger, immobilization is key.

Symptoms A cut, bruise, lump, or depression on scalp. Possible unconsciousness, confusion, or drowsiness. Bleeding from the nose, ear, or mouth. Pale or reddish face. Headache. Vomiting. Convulsions. Pupils in eyes unequal in size. Difficulty in speech. Confusion. Change in pulse rate.

Treatment
- ABC procedure.

- Keep player lying down and quiet. If movement of player is necessary, handle player carefully. There may be a neck injury as well.

- If there is no evidence of neck or back injury, turn the player's head to the side to allow secretions to drain.

- Control serious bleeding with direct pressure to the bleeding area.

- *Do not* give the player anything by mouth.

- Seek medical attention promptly. If someone other than a trained EMS unit must move the player, transport the patient lying down and with pads on each side of the head to keep it from moving from side to side.

Injury Neck injury

Cause Neck injury should be suspected if a head injury has occurred. *Never* move a player with a suspected neck injury without trained medical assistance unless the player is in imminent danger of death.

Symptoms Head injury. Headache. Stiff neck. Inability to move. Inability to move specific parts of the body, such as arms or legs. Tingling sensation in feet and hands.

Treatment   Immobilize the neck with a rolled towel or newspaper about 4 inches wide wrapped around the neck and tied loosely in place.

- ABC procedure.

- Summon paramedics or trained medical professionals immediately.

- Lay folded towels, blankets, clothing, or other suitable objects around the player's head, neck, and shoulders to keep the head and neck from moving. Place bricks or stones next to the blankets for additional support.

- Keep the player warm.

Injury   Nosebleed

Causes   Blow to the nose. Scratching the nose. Repeated nose blowing. Infection.

Symptoms   Bleeding. Swelling. Pain. Deformity of the nose.

Treatment
- Have player sit down and lean forward, keeping mouth open so that blood or clots will not obstruct airway.

- Squeeze sides of the nose together for about 15 minutes. (Squeeze the nose below the bone, not on top of the nose.)

- Release slowly. *Do not* allow player to blow or touch the nose.

- If bleeding continues, squeeze the nose closed again for 5 minutes.

- Place a cold cloth or ice in a cloth against the player's nose and face to help constrict the blood vessels.

- If bleeding continues, seek medical attention.

- Seek medical attention if you suspect a broken nose.

- *Do not* let player irritate or blow nose for several hours after the bleeding has stopped.

Injury	Laceration (cut or tear of the skin)
Causes	Direct blows to the body. Falls. Collisions.
Symptoms	Bleeding. Swelling.

Treatment
- Wash hands thoroughly with soap and water before treating the wound.

- If cut is bleeding, apply direct pressure over the wound with a sterile or clean cloth.

- When bleeding has stopped, wash the wound with soap and water to remove dirt or foreign materials near the skin's surface. *Do not* attempt to remove foreign material that is deeply embedded in tissue; serious bleeding may result.

- Rinse the wound thoroughly under running water.

- Pat wound dry with a sterile or clean cloth.

- *Do not* apply ointments, medication, or antiseptic spray unless told to do so by a doctor.

- Cover the wound with sterile dressing and bandage in place.

- *Always* seek medical attention when any of the following conditions exists:

Wound is severe.

Bleeding does not stop.

Foreign material/object is embedded in the wound.

There are signs of infection: fever, redness, swelling, increased tenderness at wound site, or pus.

There is any doubt about tetanus immunization.

Injury Broken bone

(A break or crack in a bone is a fracture. Fractures are closed or open. In closed fractures, the broken bone does not come through the skin. In an open fracture, there is an open wound that extends down to the bone. An open break is more serious due to severe bleeding.)

Causes Direct blows. Falls. Collisions.

Symptoms Player feels or hears a bone snap. Injury site is painful or tender, especially to the touch. Difficulty moving the injured part. The injured part moves abnormally or unnaturally. Swelling in area of the injury. Injured part is deformed. Site of injury shows a bluish discoloration.

Treatment
- Stop any severe bleeding.
- *Do not* try to push back any part of the bone that is sticking out.
- *Do not* wash the wound or insert anything into it.
- Gently apply pressure with a large sterile or clean pad to stop the bleeding, if any.
- Cover entire wound with bandage.
- Treat for shock.
- Call for paramedics.
- Handle player very gently.
- *Do not* give the player anything to eat or drink.

<h1>CHAPTER 5</h1>

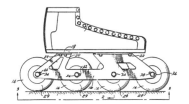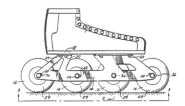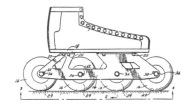

FITNESS

Stretching

In-line hockey is a sport of explosive motions and frequent changes in direction. And like a great many other competitive sports, it should include a thorough warm-up and cool-down period prior to each game or practice. An effective warm-up routine will prepare your muscle groups for quick and intense bursts of movement and reduce the possibility of muscle and/or soft-tissue injury. This is best accomplished by a program combining both light aerobic activity and stretching before and after a game or practice.

Why Stretch?

- Prevents injuries such as muscle strains. (A strong, stretched muscle is resilient and less likely to tear.)

- Reduces muscle tension and makes the body feel more relaxed.

- Prepares you for strenuous activity. It is a way of signaling the muscles that they are about to be used.

- Helps coordination by allowing for freer and easier movement.

- Increases your range of motion.

- Promotes circulation of blood and oxygen.

- Helps to relax the mind's control over the body.

- Develops greater body awareness. As you stretch each part of the body, you focus on them and begin to "know" them and their limitations.

- Makes you feel good.

Getting Ready

Prior to stretching, do some light skating or jogging to warm and relax your body. Five to 10 minutes should be sufficient. Find an area free of "hockey traffic" and distractions. It is best to stretch with your skates off, since they tend to get in the way.

Breathing

Breathe as you stretch. If you grit your teeth and hold your breath, a natural tendency, you block the flow of oxygen to your body. If a particular stretching position is obstructing your breathing, adjust your body position until you are relaxed and breathing normally again.

Don't Overdo It

Whenever you overstretch, you send a message to the body to contract the muscle in order to protect it from injury, since relaxed muscles are more prone to injury. Holding a stretch beyond your "ceiling of flexibility" or bouncing strains the muscle and activates what is called the "stretch reflex." It hurts and—even worse—damages the muscle by tearing microscopic tissue fibers. Just as a scar forms when you cut yourself, a muscle scars when it is damaged. Ultimately, elasticity is reduced and your muscle becomes tight and sore. Moreover, subsequent stretching becomes a loathsome experience, when in fact it should relax you and allow blood to reach your extremities.

Many of us have been misguided by the time-worn phrase "No pain, no gain." In stretching, nothing could be further from the truth. Proper stretching is not painful. Pain, in fact, should tell you something is wrong with your stretching technique or may be indicative of a previously damaged muscle or tendon. In such cases, do not hesitate to see your doctor.

Flexibility

Remember, warm muscles are more flexible than cold ones. Also, be aware that cold climates and high elevations (less oxygen) may require that you increase both your warm-up and cool-down periods.

Flexibility is developed and maintained through an ongoing stretching routine. Stretching serves three functions: first, to prepare the body for a game, practice, or workout session; second, to develop overall body flexibility; and third, to cool down muscles after vigorous activity. Although in-line hockey does not have an "off-season" per se, it is advisable to continue a stretching program year-round to improve and maintain flexibility.

Stretching exercises for both the lower and upper body should be done for a minimum of 10 minutes prior to each workout, followed by 10 to 15 minutes afterward. For young players, or those who are well conditioned or very flexible, these exercise guidelines should be quite safe. Those getting back into the swing of things following an injury or a long period of inactivity should take care not to lock (or hyperextend) joints, since this places stress on the back, hips, neck, and knees.

Stretching Exercises

Head Rolls

Benefit

This exercise improves neck flexibility and also helps to tone and strengthen the muscles in the neck.

Technique

1. Assume a standing position with your arms at your sides.

2. Roll your head around your chest, shoulders, and back in both directions.

3. Flex your head forward by dropping your chin downward as far as possible.

4. Extend your head as far backward as possible.

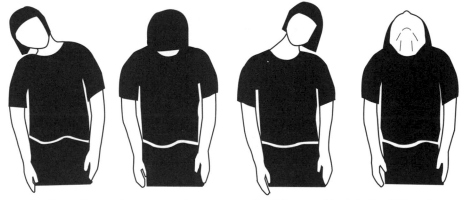

Head Rolls. Roll your head around your chest, shoulders, and back in both directions.

Standing Side-to-Side Stretch. Bend sideways at the waist, and move your arms to the same side.

Standing Side-to-Side Stretch

Benefit

This exercise will stretch your arms, shoulders, and sides.

Technique

1. Stand with your feet about shoulder-width apart.

2. Extend your arms straight overhead.

3. Bend sideways at the waist, and move your arms to the same side until you feel a comfortable stretch through your waist and side.

Standing Shoulder Stretch. Pulling your right elbow behind your head, bend to the left side.

Standing Shoulder Stretch

Benefit

This exercise loosens the arms, shoulders, and sides. Very important for the extended backstroke used during a slap shot.

Technique

1. Standing position. Feet at shoulder width. Knees slightly bent.

2. Pull right elbow behind head, bend to the left side.

3. Hold bent position for about 10 to 15 seconds.

4. Switch to left elbow and bend to the right side.

Standing Calf Stretch

Benefit

This exercise increases flexibility and circulation in the legs, particularly the Achilles tendon—the muscle between your ankle and the back of your knee.

 It is essential to keep the heel of the back leg firmly planted on the ground, with your toes slightly turned as you hold the stretch.

Technique

1. Stand a small distance from a wall or post, and lean into it with your forearms.

2. Rest your head on your hands.

3. Bend one leg, and place your foot on the ground in front of you, extending the other leg straight behind you.

4. Slowly move the hips forward, keeping the lower back flat.

5. Do two sets and repeat with the other leg.

Standing Calf Stretch. Stand a small distance from a wall or post, and lean into it with your forearms.

Bent Knee Standing Stretch. Assume a bent-knee position with your heels flat on the ground, toes pointed straight ahead, and feet about shoulder-width apart.

Bent Knee Standing Stretch

Benefit

In this position, you are tightening the quadriceps and relaxing the hamstrings.

Technique

1. Assume a bent-knee position with your heels flat on the ground, toes pointed straight ahead, and feet about shoulder-width apart.

2. As you hold this bent-knee position, notice the difference between the front of the thigh and the back of the thigh.

3. The quadriceps (front) should be firm and tight, while the hamstring (back) should feel soft and relaxed.

Sitting Hamstring Stretch

Benefit

This exercise stretches the hamstrings.

Technique

1. Sit with your right leg straight and the sole of your left foot slightly touching the inside of the right thigh. You are now in a straight-leg, bent-knee position.

2. Slowly bend forward from the hips toward the foot of the straight leg until you feel tension. As the tension diminishes, bend a little more and hold.

3. During this stretch, keep the foot of your straight leg upright, relaxing your ankle and toes.

 Are you remembering to breathe as you stretch? Don't grit your teeth or hold your breath. Always relax and breathe easily.

Sitting Hamstring Stretch (step 1)

Sitting Hamstring Stretch (step 2)

4. Be sure that the quadriceps is relaxed during this stretch. If you cannot easily reach your feet, use a towel to help you stretch.

Sitting Spine Twist

Benefit

This exercise helps prepare your body for side-to-side movement. Stretches the lower back and sides of the hips.

Technique

1. Sitting position.

2. Extend your right leg in front of you.

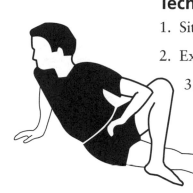

3. Lift your left leg up and cross it over your right knee. (Your left foot should rest on the outside of your right knee.)

4. Rest your bent, left elbow just above your left knee.

5. Place your right hand behind you for balance.

6. Look over your right shoulder. At the same time, rotate your upper body in the same direction.

7. Hold the stretch for 10 to 15 seconds, and switch sides.

Do not push on your knees! Bend from the hips until you feel a mild tension and hold.

An alternative method, if you have trouble balancing, is to sit against a wall or couch. With your back straight and the soles of your feet together, use your hands to push gently downward on the insides of your thighs.

Sitting Groin Stretch

Benefit

This exercise increases flexibility in the groin. Especially important for goaltenders, who are called on to perform split and butterfly saves.

Technique

1. Place the soles of your feet together and hold your toes.

2. Gently pull yourself forward, bending from the hips, until you feel a little tension in your groin.

3. Try placing your elbows on the outside of your legs and slowly bend the spine downward. Do not bounce. Do two sets and remember to breathe.

Sitting Groin Stretch

Complete the exercise by moving your head through a slow circle, reaching it toward your right knee—between your legs—toward your left knee—and finally, sit up straight. Continue this exercise in a circular manner; then repeat the cycle in the opposite direction. Move in a slow circle and do not bounce. This exercise also loosens the waist and back muscles.

Groin/Hips Stretch

Benefit

This exercise stretches the inner thighs, groin, and hips. Especially helpful for side-to-side movement and flexibility.

Technique

1. Sit on the floor and spread your legs as wide apart as you can comfortably.

2. Place your hands on your legs or feet, and stretch your head toward the floor between your legs.

3. Now place both hands on your right leg or foot and reach your head toward your right knee.

4. Repeat on your left leg or foot.

Groin/Hips Stretch
(side view)

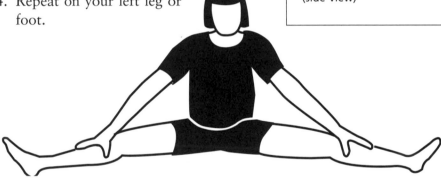

Groin/Hips Stretch (frontal view)

Lower Back and Side Stretch

Benefit

This exercise is very helpful for stretching the entire lumbar region of the body.

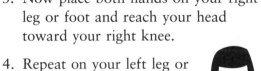

Lower Back and Side
Stretch (frontal view)

Make sure the back, head, shoulders, and elbows remain flush to the floor. This helps to maximize the stretch.

Technique

1. Start with feet resting on the floor.

2. Lift the left leg over the right.

3. Pull the right leg downward until you feel the side of your hip and lower back being stretched.

4. Hold this position for 30 seconds.

Back of Neck Stretch

Benefit

This exercise reduces tension and increases circulation in the upper spinal column and neck.

Technique

1. Begin from a lying position.

2. Clasp fingers behind your head.

3. As though you were beginning a sit-up, pull your head forward with your arms.

4. Hold for 10 seconds.

5. Repeat several times.

Back of Neck Stretch (back view)

Lower Back Stretch

Benefit

This exercise further stretches the groin, and is a very relaxing position.

Technique

1. Begin in the first position.

Lower Back Stretch (step 1)

2. Bend the knees and place the soles of your feet together.

3. Hold for up to 30 seconds.

4. Relax.

Lower Back Stretch (step 2)

Squat

Benefit

This exercise stretches a number of areas, including the lower legs, knees, back, ankles, tendons, and groin.

Technique

1. Begin from a standing position.

2. Keeping the back straight, bend at the knees into a squatting position.

3. Keep your heels flat on the floor and point your toes slightly outward.

4. Maintain this position for up to 30 seconds.

Achilles Stretch

Benefit

This exercise increases the flexibility and resiliency of the Achilles tendon. You may not realize it with those skate boots on, but the Achilles tendon is always being worked while skating—particularly when you are carving out those C cuts.

Apply gentle pressure whenever flexing the Achilles tendon. It can be easily strained.

Technique

1. Begin with one knee on the floor.

2. Place the toes of your other leg even with your knee.

3. Reach forward with your legs and torso, while keeping the heel of your bent leg on the floor.

4. Hold for up to 10 seconds.

Achilles Stretch. Your heel must remain flat to the surface for the stretch to be effective.

Front of Hip/Hamstring Stretch

Benefit

This exercise increases the flexibility in the front of the hip, the hamstring, and the groin.

This exercise places significant pressure on your forward knee. If you have knee problems, pay particular attention to any pain. If you do feel pain, do not continue. Your knees are very fragile, so take special care of them.

Technique

1. To stretch the hamstring, move one leg forward until the knee of the forward leg is directly over the ankle.

2. Rest your other knee on the ground.

Front of Hip/Hamstring Stretch

3. Without changing the position of the knee on the ground or the front foot, slowly lower the front of your hip downward.

Forearms and Wrists Stretch

Benefit

This is a very helpful stretch, since so much of passing and shooting uses the muscles in the forearms and wrists.

Technique

1. Begin on your hands and knees.

2. Place the palms of your hands on the floor so that your fingertips are pointing to your knees and your thumbs are facing outward.

3. Hold this position for 20 seconds.

4. Repeat.

Forearms and Wrists Stretch. A very helpful stretch for the shooting and passing of in-line roller hockey.

Full Body Stretch

Benefit

This exercise stretches a number of major muscles all at once, including those in the feet, ankles, arms, shoulders, spine, abdomen, and rib cage.

Technique

1. Lie on the floor, chest facing up.

2. Extend your arms and legs in opposite directions.

3. Stretch and hold for 5 seconds.

4. Relax and repeat.

Feet

Benefit

Feet are often neglected. They bear the weight of our bodies for a lifetime, so they need special attention. This exercise helps to increase the circulation in your feet.

Technique

1. Lie flat on your back (this is great to do before you get out of bed in the morning) and extend your toes as far as they will go.

2. Imagine stretching for a one-hundred-dollar bill that is just out of reach.

3. You should feel tension across the top of each foot.

Ankles

Benefit

This exercise helps to stretch tight ligaments and tendons.

Technique

1. While sitting up, rotate your ankles clockwise and counterclockwise through a complete circle of motion.

2. Provide slight resistance with your hand.

3. Repeat 10 to 20 times in each direction.

Toes

Benefit

This exercise will stretch the upper tendons of the foot.

Technique

1. Use your fingers to pull your toes gently toward you.

2. Pull the toes in the opposite direction to stretch the upper tendons of the foot.

3. Hold each stretch for 10 seconds and repeat three times.

Sole of Foot

Benefit

This exercise will relax the foot and help to improve blood circulation.

Technique

1. With the flat part of your fist, gently strike in rapid succession the sole of the foot, moving vigorously from heel to toe.

2. Repeat on the opposite foot.

Every human body is unique and requires different stretches. You know your body better than anyone else. If you feel tightness somewhere, do what feels right—slowly and without bouncing.

Your muscles need time to wake up just as you do. A complete stretching routine should be completed before and after each game or practice. Neglecting a proper warm-up or stretching routine is one of the most common causes of avoidable injury.

<h1>Chapter 6</h1>

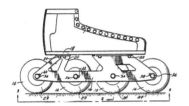 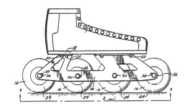 

Skills & Drills

The fundamental techniques of in-line roller hockey cannot be properly learned from a book, any more than a surgeon can learn his craft from a medical text. A manual simply cannot replace a qualified coach or instructor. What follows is intended as an introduction to and a conceptual framework for some of the basic skills used to play in-line roller hockey.

Balance and Stability

A balanced center of gravity is the foundation for all in-line skating activities, roller hockey included. To maintain your center, keep your knees bent over the toes and ankles flexed forward. Your back should be straight, your stomach in, your shoulders square, your head up, and your eyes open. *Do not* stare at your skates, the stick's blade, or the puck. As you race from one end of the rink to the other, your world will be flashing by like images through a train window. Keep your eyes moving!

How to Fall

You *will* fall. Everyone does. The most common contact areas are the wrists, shoulders, tailbone, elbows, knees, and head. Fortunately, manufacturers of protective equipment know this and design gear with those vulnerable areas in mind. However, there is a very obvious key point to be made here with respect to gear: *You must wear it.*

The proper way to fall is head first. (Note: This does not mean on your head!) I know. Sounds crazy, doesn't it? It may be difficult at first, but you must learn to develop confidence in your equipment. And because we all have a sense of balance, we have to overcome our natural reluctance to fall. The best way to do that is to practice. Yes, actually practice falling.

The first step in learning to fall properly is to relax. Tense muscles tear. The next thing you should do is lower your center of gravity by bending your knees. This will shorten the distance you have to fall. And last, the fall itself: Try to collapse your body so that the impact is directed toward your protected areas—wrists, elbows, knees, in that order. Falling straight onto your knees often works well too. The key, again, is to relax and roll (if you must) until you have dissipated your momentum. Continue to practice falling until you don't have to think about it. In a "live" situation, you won't have time.

Whenever possible, "guide" your fall so that your protective gear absorbs the shock.

In-line Roller Hockey Ready Position

Always bend with your knees. If you can see your skates while looking down, you are not bending enough. An indicator of proper technique: quadriceps are sore after your first few games.

Overview

The in-line roller hockey ready position is the foundation on which every other in-line roller hockey skill is based. From this position you can move quickly and in control in any direction. I call this the basic ready position, or "BRP," and will refer to it as such throughout this chapter.

Technique

1. Skates are shoulder-width apart.

2. Weight is on inside edges of skates.

3. Knees are bent over the toes.

4. Back and chest are up. Head is up and facing forward.

5. Shoulders are level and in line with the knees and toes.

6. Stick blade is held flush against the surface.

7. Both hands are on stick, ready to receive a pass.

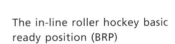

The in-line roller hockey basic ready position (BRP)

Common Mistakes

* Positioning your skates too wide or too close. This reduces your stability and quickness.

* Bending too much at the waist. Don't hunch over. This straightens the knees and reduces your stability.

* Leaning on the stick for balance.

Bent knee over the toe is one of the most fundamental techniques in in-line roller hockey. If you can see your toe when looking down, you probably are not bending enough.

Warm-Up Drills

Windmill, or Twists

Benefit

A useful pre-practice/game warm-up exercise. Loosens the upper body, including the neck, back, and waist.

Technique

1. Glide on both skates.

2. Hockey stick rests behind your neck. Each wrist is draped over stick shaft.

3. Twist side-to-side and dip up-and-down.

Toe Touch

Benefit

A useful pre-practice/game warm-up exercise. Helps with balance while stretching the back, legs, and arms.

The Windmill Drill helps to loosen the upper body, including the neck, back, and waist.

 Perform this exercise slowly so as not to strain your back.

Technique

1. Glide on both skates.

2. Feet are slightly wider than shoulder width.

3. Hold stick with two hands on the stick's blade. Stick is held out and in front of the body.

4. Bend at the waist, reach down with stick, and touch toes of skates without bending the knees.

The Toe Touch Drill helps to improve your balance and edge control while also stretching the back, legs, and arms.

Leg Lift

Benefit

A useful pre-practice/game warm-up exercise. Helps with balance while loosening the lower body, including the hamstrings, quadriceps, and groin.

- Start slow and easy.
- Stay balanced at all times.
- Work toward touching the stick with your skate.

Technique

1. Glide on both skates.

2. Hold stick horizontally at shoulder height.

The Leg Lift Drill helps to improve your balance and flexibility in the leg muscles.

3. Shift weight to either skate and glide on that skate.

4. At the same time, lift other leg up toward the stick.

5. Alternate between glide leg and lift leg.

Common Errors

• Kicking leg up versus lifting it.

• Lowering the stick. Keep it at shoulder level.

Forward Dip

Benefit

A useful pre-practice/game warm-up exercise. Stretches the groin while improving balance and proper knee bend.

Technique

1. Begin by gliding on both skates.

2. Shift weight to either skate and bend deeply at the knee.

3. At the same time, extend and drag other leg behind you.

4. Stick should be held in front of you with one hand, leading your glide direction.

5. Alternate between legs.

Common Errors

• Leaning forward.

• Bouncing.

Other Warm-Up Drills

• Keep both skates on the skating surface and alternate cutting C's. This exercise emphasizes the importance of edge control when skating on in-lines.

• Keep both skates on the surface and cut hourglasses.

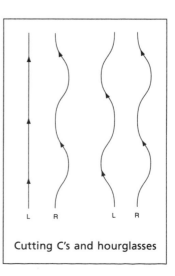

Cutting C's and hourglasses

The heel-brake technique will not be covered in this book. The heel brake can be used as a way of moderating your speed, but it is not appropriate as a stopping technique. In fact, most (if not all) skilled in-line roller hockey players remove the heel brake altogether. If you don't understand how to heel-brake properly, you're not ready to learn any other speed-control techniques.

- If drag skate is less or greater than 90 degrees (i.e., perpendicular) to the lead (glide) skate, you will twist out of control. Think more of dragging the heel than the toe.
- Increase angle of wheel edges by bending at the knees more.

- Keep both skates close together on the surface and twist back and forth as if you were skating through slalom cones.

Stopping/Speed Control Techniques

You cannot play in-line hockey until you have learned to stop. There are several stopping techniques.

T-Stop

Overview

Used primarily for speed control or for a low-speed, rolling stop. The T-stop is *not* the most appropriate stopping technique. It is, however, an effective method for moderating speed on the skating surface.

Technique

1. Legs are parallel. Back is straight and squared to the skating direction.

2. While skating forward, scissor skates so that one of the skates is slightly ahead of the other.

3. Lift and turn one skate 90 degrees (toe pointing outward). Lay down the inside edge of that skate on the surface behind the glide skate.

4. Keep most of your weight on the front (glide) skate.

5. Increase pressure on rear (drag) skate until you slow down or stop.

Common Errors

- Gliding straight.

- Drag skate buckles and kicks off the surface.

Snow Plow

Overview

Good technique for low-speed, rolling stop.

The snow plow stop requires that you press against the inside edge of your skates. It is best used for a low-speed, rolling stop.

 If you have ever snow-skied, the concepts are the same—except there is no snow.

Technique

1. Knees are bent. Weight is forward.

2. Point toes slightly inward.

3. Press against the inside edges of skates.

4. Rock (or waddle) from skate to skate as you go, especially when stopping from higher speeds.

Common Errors

• Toes pointed inward too much.

• Leaning back on heels.

Hockey Stop

Overview

Very effective stop for high speeds, but difficult to master. Similar to power (or control) turn, but with slight modifications.

Hockey stop

Technique

1. Begin by starting a power (or control) turn. (See below.)

2. When entering turn, swing outside leg into a very tight C arc. If turning to the left, lead with right leg. The back leg follows.

 • Lean into the direction of the turn.
• "Think" about the direction you want to turn. Your body has an innate sense of direction—tell it where you want it to go.
• Tighten the arc to quicken the stop.

3. Shift weight from inner skate to outer skate. This shift will transfer your weight to the inside edge of the outside skate, resulting in a stop.

Common Error

• Dipping inner shoulder. Keep it upright.

Power Slide

Overview

Very effective stop for high speeds, but difficult to master and wears down wheels quickly.

- Visualize that you are shaving a thin layer of ice with your extended, sliding leg.

- Increase flex in the right leg. This lowers the angle of your wheel edges, which helps prevent them from "catching" on the surface. Especially important on rougher, grippier surfaces like asphalt.

Technique

1. From forward stride, pivot right skate (toe pointing outward) so the heel is pointing in your skating direction. Simultaneously, swing the left skate around. You are now facing backward.

2. Keep right leg bent. Extend left leg backward.

3. Lay down the wheel edges of the left skate against the surface, and slide until you stop.

Common Error

- Wheel edges of slide leg "catch" on the skating surface.

Power Slide

Backward Stopping

Snow Plow

Overview

Good technique for low-speed, rolling stop.

Technique

1. While skating backward, lean slightly forward.

2. Turn knee and toe of skates outward, heels inward.

3. Put pressure on inside edges of skates to stop.

Mohawk Turn, or Turning Forward to Backward

Overview

In in-line roller hockey the ability to change skating directions quickly and efficiently is essential.

Technique

1. Bring stick close in to the body.

2. While skating forward, lift and turn the left foot (if turning to the left). For a brief moment, your skates will be heel-to-heel, with the toes facing in opposite directions.

3. As you place your left foot on the surface, the pivot (or right foot, in this example) should turn slightly in the same direction.

Try practicing without a stick so you can concentrate on the footwork.

Mohawk turn

Common Error

• Failing to hold the stick with two hands, which results in the stick ending up behind you and out of control.

Moving Forward

V-Start

Overview

This will help you accelerate quickly from a stationary (standing) position.

Technique

1. BRP.

2. Turn toes outward. Your feet should form a V shape.

3. Thrust off the inside edge of either skate. Thrust back and to the side.

The V-start requires that you thrust off the inside edge of either skate.

4. Glide leg is bent over the toe.

5. Completely extend thrust leg. Drive completely through the end of the stroke, snapping the heel (not the toe) outward.

6. After a few strokes, transition into a regular skating stride.

Common Errors

• "Flicking" your toe out at the end of each skate stroke. Not driving completely through the last wheel of the skate. Very common among less-advanced skaters.

• Bending over at the waist.

 Imagine digging in with edge of skate wheels. Edge should form a 45-degree angle to the surface.

Side (Lateral) Start

Overview

This will help you move quickly in either direction.

Technique

1. BRP.

2. Look toward direction you want to skate.

3. Pivot either foot in the same direction.

The side start is used to start skating to your left or your right.

4. Drive off the inside edge of your opposite skate.

5. Make a few quick strides, then transition to regular skating stride.

Common Error

- Stronger starting one way than the other. You will not always have the choice of moving toward your dominant (preferred) side. Be strong starting in either direction.

Penguin Walk

Benefit

Effective (and silly looking) drill to develop proper skate angle and edge control when starting.

This is a stepping motion. You should not glide when skate contacts the ground.

Technique

1. Heels together, toes apart. Forms a V shape.

2. Knees bent and turned out.

3. Walk (or waddle) on edges of skate with wheels at 45-degree angle.

Forward Crossover

Overview

A fundamental skating technique for skating forward. It is especially useful in in-line roller hockey, because you can increase your speed while turning.

Technique

The entire movement should be smooth and continuous. Practice skating in both directions (i.e., clockwise and counter-clockwise).

1. Upper body should be up, the knees bent, weight slightly forward.

2. Stroke (push) with your right (or left) foot, to the side and slightly back.

3. When your right foot is fully extended, swing it out, around, and place it down and directly ahead of your left skate.

4. Simultaneously, push off with your left skate (now under the right).

Forward crossover

Turning

Control Turn (Turning Left)

Overview

This exercise helps you to turn quickly and in control.

Think "turn left" (really, it helps!).

Technique

1. BRP as you approach turning point.

2. Lead with left skate. Weight should be on outside edges. Knee bent over the toe.

3. Trail with right skate. Weight on inner edges.

4. Rotate hips and torso in direction of the turn.

Common Errors

• Do not dip your shoulder into the turn. It puts you out of balance.

Crossover Turn (Turning Left)

Overview

Like the crossover stride, the crossover turn is especially useful in in-line roller hockey, since you can actually accelerate while turning.

Keep the knees bent over the toe. You should not be able to see the toe of your skate if this is done properly.

Technique

1. Thrust off the inside edge of the right leg.

2. Place the weight on the outer edge of the left skate.

3. Cross the left skate up, around, and slightly behind the right leg.

4. Extend the left leg completely, then return the left skate to its original position.

Common Error

• Not completely extending the driving leg of each stride.

Backward Skating

Snowplow

Overview

If you have not played any type of hockey before, you have never had a real need to skate backward. You must be able to skate backward to play in-line roller hockey well. If you cannot skate backward proficiently, it is time to learn how.

• Think "bend at the knee, then cut a C."

• Hold stick with one hand so you can effectively poke-check when playing defense.

• Most backward skating is done by using the inside edges of skates.

Technique

1. From a heel-out/toe-in position, push off the inner edge of your skate.

2. Push and extend the thrust leg. Bend at the knee on the glide leg.

3. Fully extend the stroking leg, then bring it back to its original position.

Common Errors

• Weight is too far forward.

• Skates are less than (less stable) or greater than (less power) shoulder width.

Stickhandling

Grip

Overview

One of the most important components of puck control is the positioning of the hands on the stick.

- Imagine gripping the stick as though you had two fingers, like a crab's claw.
- Always wear gloves when practicing. Without protective gloves, the feel of the stick is drastically different.

Technique

1. BRP.

2. Place the left hand (for right-handers) on the top of the stick's shaft, just below the knob (or "butt end") of the stick.

3. Lower hand is spaced between 16 and 18 inches from the knob.

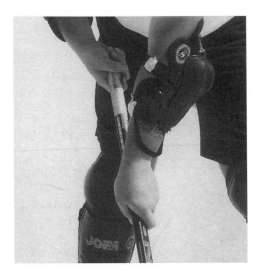

Proper grip of the hockey stick. The thumb and index finger should form a "V" around the shaft.

4. The grip should form a V shape, with the thumb and forefinger of each hand on the top side of the shaft.

5. Head is up. Don't look at the puck.

6. Hold stick in front of the body.

7. Relax elbows and shoulders. This allows them to move freely.

8. "Cup" the puck by rolling the wrists toward the surface.

Common Errors

- Hands too close together on stick.

- Arms too close to body.

- Gripping the stick too tightly or with the palms.

- Slapping at the puck versus "pushing" it.

- Using the arms rather than the wrists to move the puck.

- Looking down at the puck. Glimpse it peripherally, but don't look at it. With your head up, you see the entire rink.

Puck Control

Overview

Along with the skates, a stick is an in-line roller hockey player's most "personal" piece of equipment. Your stick should become part of you—an extension of your arm. Hold and wield it as much as possible. Always have a stick nearby. Hold it while you watch TV or talk on the phone. During the playing season, make it a daily part of your life.

Cupping the puck with the curved face of the blade

Technique

• Build wrist and forearm strength. Very important. Take a tennis ball (or other wrist-strengthening device) wherever you go. You don't have to set aside special time to do this. Build strength while reading, walking to school, or talking on the telephone.

1. Hold the stick in front of the body. The elbows should be able to move freely back and forth. Each time you move the puck from one point to another, roll the wrists toward the surface.

2. Keep the backswing short and quick. Big backswings alert the goaltender to an impending shot.

3. In heavy traffic, keep the puck close to the body. Make it tougher for defenders to knock away. Also, keep the puck in front of you. From this "neutral" position you are able to move in any direction.

Cupping the puck with the backhand side of the blade

• Practice until you get a "feel" for the puck. Practice flipping a ball (with the stick's blade turned up). Bounce it up and down. Walk around with it.

4. Think of pushing and pulling the puck—*not* slapping it.

Dribbling and Advancing the Puck

Overview

Moving the puck from one end of the rink to the other is a basic skill in in-line roller hockey. Imagine, if you will, trying to play basketball without dribbling. Or baseball without throwing. Or soccer without kicking. Get the idea? In-line hockey moves so quickly that you cannot concentrate on basic stick-handling and the game at the same time. Be the best in-line roller hockey player you can by practicing this drill properly and often.

If there is open surface ahead, try shoveling (pushing motion) the puck a few yards ahead at a time, then catch up to it. This helps you gain speed while skating. Especially effective in a breakaway situation.

• Start with a standing drill until you have the technique, then put the two together—skating and dribbling—at the same time.

• As skills improve, extend the width of the puck motion.

• Practice often, until the puck feels like an extension of your hands.

• Practice almost anywhere. It doesn't take a lot of space, or a partner, or rink facilities to improve. A little space in your bedroom, a ball, and a stick is all you need.

Technique

1. Keep the puck in front of you as you move about the rink.

2. Keep the puck within range. Don't let it get too far ahead of you.

3. When starting from a standing, stationary position, shovel (push) the puck in the direction of travel a short distance. This allows you to explode into your skating stride without carrying the puck.

4. Don't look at the puck. Develop a "feel" for it and a sense of where it is. Develop your peripheral vision.

Common Mistakes

• Looking at the puck. This can be especially dangerous when skating through congested areas.

• Kicking the puck with your skate(s).

• Letting the puck fall behind and "dragging" it. With the puck out in front of your skating path, you have a better sense of its position.

Dribbling Drills
Lateral, or Side-to-Side Dribble

Overview

The lateral (or side-to-side) dribble, the most common dribbling technique, is used to move the puck from side to side in front of the body.

Technique

1. BRP.

2. Puck-control fundamentals.

3. Move the puck from side to side between 18 and 24 inches in front of the body.

4. Cup the puck with the stick's blade by rolling the wrists toward the surface.

Lateral (or side-to-side) dribble

Common Mistakes

- Slapping at the puck rather than pushing it.
- Clenching the stick tightly with the palms.
- Arms held too close to the body.
- Looking at the puck.

Forward-to-Backward (or Front-to-Back) Dribble

Overview

The forward-to-backward (or front-to-back) dribble is useful when engaging a defensive player who is moving toward you or for setting up a shot.

Technique

1. BRP.
2. Puck-control fundamentals.
3. Puck motion is at your side (i.e., parallel to your skate direction).
4. Practice on both the left and right sides of your body.

Common Mistakes

- Puck motion in front versus the side of the body.
- Puck veers into skating path.

- Start with a standing drill until you have the technique; then put the two together—skating and dribbling—at the same time.
- When an opponent is near, move the puck to the outside (the side opposite the opponent).
- Sometimes increasing the width of your grip will help with persistent puck-control problems. This adjustment can also be made when handling the puck on your weaker side.

Front-to-back dribble

Diagonal Dribble

Overview

The diagonal dribble is effective when combined with the lateral or forward-to-backward dribble.

Technique

1. Move the puck as far forward as possible.
2. Roll the wrists to cup the puck with the blade.
3. Pull the puck, don't slap at it.

Lateral (or side-to-side) dribble

• Start with a standing drill until you have the technique, then put the two together—skating and dribbling—at the same time.

• Remember, a soft touch is the key to good puck control. "Give" a little as you receive, and "cup" the puck.

• Combining this dribble with the lateral dribble and forward-to-backward dribble will provide you with the skills to fake out your opponent in a variety of situations.

Common Mistakes

• Not cupping the puck with the stick blade.

• Head is down, looking at the puck.

• Slapping at the puck.

Defensive Stick Checking
Poke Check

Overview

The poke check is an effective stick-checking technique when the defender is skating backward in front of an advancing puck carrier. Used to knock the puck from the opponent's stick.

Technique

1. Stick hand is held close to body.

2. Elbow is bent.

3. Quickly extend arm and stick toward the puck. Use the full length of the shaft up to the knob. (This is performed with one hand.)

Common Errors

• The defender's checking arm starts from an extended position.

• The defender lunges at the puck and is put out of balance.

The poke check is used when the defender is skating backward in front of an advancing puck/ball carrier.

- Imagine throwing your elbow at the puck.
- Make sure you have a knob on the end of your stick's shaft so the stick will not slide through your hands.

- Using two hands. The poke check cannot be properly executed with two hands on the stick.

Lift Check

Overview

The lift check is an effective stick-checking technique when the defender approaches the opponent from behind. Used to lift the stick in the air to steal the puck away.

Technique

1. Approach the puck carrier from behind.

2. Skate with the puck carrier.

3. When close enough, reach and lift your stick under opponent's.

4. Bring down your stick to the surface and steal puck away.

Common Errors

- Reaching, but not lifting, opponent's stick.

- Failing to continue skating, making it difficult to gain position on your opponent.

Sweep Check

Overview

An effective method of stick checking, this involves "sweeping" your stick low to the ground and knocking the stick (and the puck) away from an opponent.

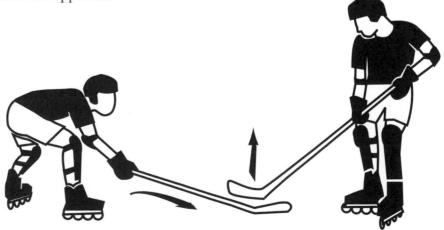

The sweep check—an effective way to knock the puck/ball from your opponent.

Most players draw the puck better from the backhand than the forehand.

Each referee has a unique style of dropping the puck. This is their prerogative, just as you have your own playing style. Take mental notes on each referee's dropping technique. Some will "drop" the puck so hard that it bounces up. Remember, anticipation is half the battle.

In a way, the face-off is analogous to the head-to-head confrontation between batters and pitchers in baseball. It is a battle of wits that requires that you think (or guess) better than your opponent. Remember, each time you "strike out" you should still learn something about your opponent, the way the referee drops the puck, and perhaps even the way the puck bounces on your playing surface.

Technique

1. Approach the puck carrier.

2. Skate with the puck carrier.

3. When close enough, bend at the knees and waist and with an arcing/sweeping motion hit your opponent's stick.

4. Recover to upright position and steal puck away.

Common Error

• Reaching with the stick as opposed to using a wide sweeping motion.

Face-Off

Overview

Every action in in-line roller hockey—every pass, every shot—begins with a face-off.

During the course of a game, face-offs represent dozens of opportunities to take possession of the puck. Like all other skills, becoming a proficient face-off artist requires practice. Everyone on the team should develop at least some knowledge of the technique.

Technique

1. Whoever takes the draw (i.e., the one who faces off) is responsible for assuring that his teammates are positioned properly and are prepared for play.

2. From a BRP, place your stick on the surface where the puck is to be dropped.

3. The demands of in-line roller hockey require that you be able to anticipate what you are going to do with the puck before you get

Players preparing for a face-off.

Dropping the puck in a face-off.

- Anticipating the meeting point of the puck and the receiver when passing is similar to what a quarterback must do when throwing to a receiver. Eventually, you will acquire a sense for "angling" your passes accurately.
- To increase control when passing, slide your lower hand down the stick 4–6 inches from the position used for stickhandling.
- Remember, you can always pass the puck faster than you or your opponent can skate.

- On flip or lift passes, the puck may be bouncing. Try using the face of the blade to hit the puck down and bring it under control. Keep the blade at 90 degrees to the playing surface.
- Your stick should meet the puck perpendicular to the direction of the pass.
- Passes that fall short can be retrieved on the skate wheels and kicked forward to the stick.

it. Are you going with the forehand? The backhand? Whatever you do, don't get in a rut and become predictable to your opponent.

4. Watch the puck in the referee's hand as he prepares to drop it. Don't look at the face-off circle.

5. If your opponent is not squaring up to the face-off circle, or is otherwise interfering with your ability to, then back off from the circle. Get out of your set position and notify the referee.

Passing and Receiving

Overview

Passing and receiving are what makes in-line roller hockey a team sport—they require teamwork. Passing and receiving are also the fastest and most efficient ways to advance the puck for goal-scoring opportunities. Although there are a variety of hockey passes, they all require a set of basic skills. Mastery of these skills will ensure that a) your passes are crisp and accurate and b) your reception of passes is soft and controlled.

Technique

Passer

1. Reposition lower hand on the stick's shaft between 4 and 6 inches from the position used for stick handling.

2. Head is up and focusing on the target—the point at which the puck and receiver meet.

3. "Cup" the puck with the stick's blade.

4. Puck moves off the stick's blade from heel to toe.

5. Keep the puck on the surface with a low, sweeping follow-through. Think "Sweep-push-guide."

6. Push or snap the puck toward the target—i.e., the imaginary point at which the puck and the receiver should meet—also known as "leading the receiver." It is the passer's responsibility to anticipate the receiver's position and pass to that spot.

Receiver

1. Hold stick loosely, with the stick blade on the surface.

2. Cushion the puck by holding your stick about 12 inches in front of your skates (while standing sideways).

3. When receiving the pass (on the forehand side), cradle-and-cup the puck with the curved portion of the blade. Receiving a puck on the backhand side is a bit tricky, since there is no curve to cradle the puck. Let your stick move slightly with the momentum of the puck.

Common Errors

- Passing the puck behind the receiver.

- Receiver does not cushion puck.

- Looking down at the puck rather than up at the target.

- Passer leads the receiver into heavy traffic, making the receiver vulnerable to stick checks.

Forehand Sweep Pass

Overview

The wrist, or sweep, pass is a forehand pass based on a sweeping-pushing-guiding motion.

Technique

1. Hands are positioned 12 to 15 inches apart.

2. Puck is positioned at the side and behind your rear foot.

3. Sweep-push-guide, all in one motion, in the direction of your pass.

Common Errors

- Arms are held too closely together on the stick's shaft.

- Incomplete follow-through in the direction of the pass.

- Low wrist action. Not driving into the puck.

- Stick blade is not cupped over the puck.

Snap Pass

Overview

The snap pass is a forehand pass based, in part, on the wrist (or sweep) pass (explained above). Because of the considerable wrist strength required, this passing technique may be inappropriate for younger players.

Wrist (or sweep) pass

Repeat in your mind the following: "Look-sweep-guide."

Your follow-through will determine the height of the pass. High follow-through with stick's blade facing up forces an "air" pass. Low follow-through with the stick's blade turned down keeps the pass on (or low to) the surface.

Technique

1. Hands are positioned 12 to 15 inches apart.

2. Puck is positioned at the side and behind your rear foot.

3. Bring the stick's blade behind puck about 8 inches.

4. "Snap" the blade through the puck. Blade should strike the surface 1 to 2 inches behind the puck.

Common Errors

• Work on generating blade speed by developing strength in the wrist and arms. Think of it in these terms: puck speed equals blade speed.

• No weight transfer in the direction of the pass. Move back-to-front, driving off the back leg.

Snap pass. The blade should strike the surface a few inches behind the puck/ball.

Flip Pass

Overview

The flip pass is useful when you need to lift the puck off the surface to clear an obstacle, such as a stick or skate. This is a good option when there is heavy traffic.

Think of "getting under" the puck when executing this pass.

Technique

1. Hands are positioned 12 to 15 inches apart.

2. Puck is positioned at the side and slightly in front of the toe of your front skate.

3. The stick's blade is slightly open—*not* cupped.

4. "Snap" the blade through the puck. Follow through with upward movement of the stick's blade.

Common Error

• Not enough upward movement of the stick's blade. This is critical; it is what lifts the puck.

Backhand Pass

Overview

This pass is used when the puck is on your backhand side (i.e., left-to-right for right-handed shooters). This is typically a difficult pass to execute, especially for younger players: it feels, well, backward—as if you were a right-handed pitcher trying to throw with your left hand.

Technique

Remember, unlike forehand passes, the top hand follows the bottom hand.

1. Hands are positioned 12 to 15 inches apart.

2. Puck is positioned at the side and slightly behind the toe of your rear skate.

3. The stick's blade is cupped.

4. As in the wrist pass (see above), use the sweep-push-guide motion in the direction of your pass.

Common Error

• Not transferring your weight from the front to the back skate.

The backhand pass is used when passing the puck/ball from your backhand side.

The follow-through

Drop Pass

Overview

The drop pass is not really a pass at all, although the effect is the same. It is used to hand off the puck to a teammate approaching from behind.

- This is an easy and fun pass to practice with a teammate.
- A puck that hits the boards will rebound at an equal angle.

Technique
While skating forward, simply place the front of your stick blade in front of the puck and stop it completely.

Common Error
- Passing the puck backward to the approaching teammate. Remember, this is not a pass. Just stop the puck.

Board Pass

Overview
The board pass involves bouncing the puck off the boards and going around your opponent to pick up the puck. This pass can be used to pass to either yourself or a teammate.

Technique
1. The puck should be shot into the boards at a 45-degree angle at moderate speed.

2. Follow through by retrieving the puck on the rebound off the board.

Common Error
- Shooting the puck into the boards at an extreme angle.

The board pass can be used to pass to yourself or to a teammate.

Shooting

Overview

Playing in-line roller hockey is about scoring goals, and to score goals you need to shoot with quickness, accuracy, and strength. Take some time to learn about shooting techniques, and practice, practice, practice.

Technique

- Always follow through toward the target, and point the toe of the stick where you want the puck to go. Think "Sweep-pass-guide."

- About 65 percent of all goals scored are low and to the goaltender's stick side. Go with the odds and shoot it there.

- Wrist and snap shots are very effective. They are quick, are accurate, and leave little time for setup by the goaltender.

- Keep your head up and look for a goal opening. Scoring opportunities last a split second. Stay heads up and on the lookout.

- Practice shooting as often as you can. There are several shooting practice aids (e.g., Shot Maker and Shooter Tutor) on the market that allow you the freedom to practice just about any time in the convenience of your own backyard or in a vacant lot.

Sweep (Wrist) Shot

Overview

The wrist, or sweep, shot is a forehand shot based on a sweeping-pushing-guiding motion.

Technique

1. Hands are positioned 12 to 15 inches apart.

2. Puck is positioned at the side of and behind your rear foot.

3. Sweep-push-guide, all in one motion, in the direction of your shot.

Common Errors

- Arms are held too closely together on the stick's shaft.

- Work on generating blade speed by developing strength in the wrist and arms. Think of it this way: puck speed equals blade speed.
- Repeat in your mind the following: "Look-sweep-guide."

Wrist (or sweep) shot

- Incomplete follow-through in the direction of the shot.

- Low wrist action. Not driving into the puck.

- Stick blade is not cupped over the puck.

Snap Shot

Overview

The snap shot is a forehand shot based, in part, on both the wrist shot (explained above) and the slap shot (see below). Think of it as the "middle ground" between the two.

- No weight transfer into the direction of the shot. Move back-to-front, driving off the back leg.

- This is a very effective shot when you must shoot quickly and within the goal crease.

Technique

1. Hands are positioned 12 to 15 inches apart.

2. Puck is positioned at the side and behind your rear foot.

3. Bring the stick's blade behind puck about 8 inches.

4. "Snap" the blade through the puck. Blade should strike the surface 1 to 2 inches behind the puck.

Common Error

- Work on generating blade speed by developing strength in the wrist and arms. Think of it in these terms: puck speed equals blade speed.

Snap shot

Flip Shot

Overview

The flip shot is useful when you need to lift the puck off the surface to clear an obstacle such as a stick or skate. This is a good shot choice in the slot or goal crease when there is heavy traffic.

Technique

1. Hands are positioned 12 to 15 inches apart.

2. Puck is positioned at the side and slightly in front of the toe of your front skate.

3. The stick's blade is slightly open—*not* cupped.

Think of "getting under" the puck when executing this pass.

4. "Snap" the blade through the puck. Follow through with upward movement of the stick's blade.

Common Error

• Not enough upward movement of the stick's blade. This is critical; it is what lifts the puck.

Slap Shot

Overview

The slap shot is the most exciting and powerful of all shooting techniques. Be advised that this shot clearly "telegraphs" your intentions to the goaltender, thus allowing for more preparation in attempting to block the shot.

Technique

1. Hands are positioned an additional 10 inches or so from your usual shooting hand position.

• Practice your swing and mechanics without a puck. Have a coach or teammate watch and critique you.

• Always work on increasing wrist and forearm strength (wrist curls with dumbbells, squeezing tennis balls or putty, and so forth).

2. Puck is positioned in the middle of your stance.

3. Backswing your stick to about shoulder height.

4. Begin downward movement and shift your weight to the front skate.

Back swing

The slap shot—the most powerful shot there is

This is probably the only time when "slapping" at the puck is effective. Remember, with most stickhandling fundamentals, "slapping" is not advised.

5. About an inch before contact with the puck, the stick's blade comes in contact with the surface. Lean down into the stick's shaft. This causes it to flex. As it "straightens," it whips through the puck, generating increased velocity.

6. Follow through in the direction of the shot.

Common Errors

- Hands too close together.

- Taking your eye off the puck.

- Insufficient follow-through.

- The stick's blade strikes the surface too far in front of the puck.

Backhand Shot

Overview

This shot is used when the puck is on your backhand side (i.e., left-to-right for right-handed shooters). This is typically a difficult shot to execute.

Remember, unlike forehand shots, in this shot the top hand follows the bottom hand.

Technique

1. Hands are positioned 12 to 15 inches apart.

2. Puck is positioned at the side and slightly behind the toe of your rear skate.

The backhand shot is used when the puck/ball is on your backhand side.

The follow-through

Statistically, upward of 70 percent of goals scored are shot from in and around the slot and goal crease. The percentage of goals shot from 30 feet out or more is low.

3. The stick's blade is cupped.

4. Like the wrist shot (see above), use the sweep-push-guide motion in the direction of your shot.

Common Error

• Not transferring your weight from the front to the back skate.

Angles and Puck Placement

Overview

There is more to scoring goals than being a good technical shooter. You must also know the best shot to use in a given situation and where to place it. Learn to "read" the goalie.

Placement

There are a number of areas (or "holes") where a shot can be placed. Understanding what a goaltender must do to stop a shot will help you become a smarter shooter and help you determine the most effective placement for each shot you take.

Talk with your team's goaltender about shooting strategy. Ask questions and pose various shooting scenarios. In doing so you will begin to learn how a goaltender thinks. Keep a personal game diary. Record where successful shots were placed. With a little data, you can calculate "placement probabilities" and maximize scoring possibilities.

Low Stick Side

A shot low to the stick side is a difficult shot for the goaltender to stop. It forces the goalie to move laterally and handle the stick well.

High Stick Side

Also known as the blocker side. Placing a shot high to the stick side forces the goaltender to lift his stick and blocker.

Low Glove Side

Placing a shot low to the glove side forces the goaltender to move his feet and leg pads to get in proper position. This is difficult to do quickly.

High Glove Side

High and on the glove side is not the best place to shoot, since most goaltenders are quite effective with their catch gloves.

Between the Legs

A shot between the legs, or in the "five hole," is usually very difficult to stop. It is also difficult to place, since this hole opens up only when the goaltender is forced to move laterally. If you have a good fake shot, you often can make the goalie move, thus opening the five hole.

Goaltending

Make no mistake, goaltending is a demanding and, at times, thankless job. Listening to postgame chatter, one often hears how the goalie "won" or "lost" the game. As a team's last line of defense, a goaltender needs skill, strength, lightning-quick reflexes, courage, and concentration. And a lot of luck. There is nothing easy about stopping an object traveling upward of 90 miles per hour with only a split second to react.

Goalie crouch   Goalie crouch (side view)

Posture and Stance

Overview

The starting position for the goaltender is known as the goalie crouch.

Technique

1. Shoulder and knees are parallel.

2. Weight is on balls of feet.

3. Knees are slightly bent.

4. Chest is up and slightly bent forward at the waist.

5. Back is straight, not curved.

6. Head is up and out.

7. Leg pads are together and straight up and down.

8. Glove is open, out, and facing play.

9. Blocker is up and ready for shots made to the stick side.

10. Stick blade is positioned between, and a few inches in front of, skates. Bottom of blade is flush to the playing surface and facing the opposition's goal.

Common Errors

- Crouch is too deep.

- Glove hand hangs too low.

- Gap between leg pads.

- Stick blade is too close to skates. This decreases cushioning ability when puck strikes the stick blade, because the blade is rigid, and leads to rebounds (i.e., other shooting opportunities).

Holding the Stick

Technique

1. Place index finger on the wide portion of the blade.

2. Rotate wrist in an arcing motion to turn.

3. Index finger and thumb on blade of stick for stability and control.

Correct grip of the goaltender's stick. The index finger and the thumb (not visible) are placed on the blade of the stick.

Common Errors

- Holding the stick too tight.

- Grasping the stick with the palm on the stick's shaft instead of on the blade.

Moving

Incorrect grip of the goaltender's stick.

Overview

Contrary to popular perception, a goaltender must be a very good skater. Skating should always be a major training and conditioning element for goaltenders.

Forward

Objective

A goaltender must be able to move forward in the goal crouch position to intercept or deflect a shot on goal and to cut down the shooting angle whenever possible (see below).

Technique

1. Maintain basic goalie stance (or crouch).

2. Push off inside edge of either skate and glide in desired direction.

3. To stop, use the "snow plow." Point toes inward (heels outward), with weight on the inside edges of skates.

Backward

Objective

A goalie must be able to skate backward quickly while in the goalie crouch to guard the goal against an approaching attacker.

Technique

1. Maintain basic goalie stance.

2. Keep body square to stick carrier.

3. Push off inside edge of either skate and glide in desired direction.

4. To stop, point toes outward (heels inward), with weight on the inside edges of skates.

Lateral (Side-to-Side)

Overview

The goaltender must be able to move from side to side to guard the full width of the goal against a shot.

Technique

1. Begin from basic goalie crouch.

2. Leading with your stick, pivot your lead skate in the direction you want to go (i.e., if moving left, pivot left foot so that toe is facing to the left).

3. Push off the edge of your back skate.

4. Slow or stop yourself by dragging edge of trailing skate.

Common Errors

- Not pivoting the lead foot. Goaltenders with lots of ice hockey experience will need to get used to pivoting the lead skate, which they are not required to do on slick ice.

- Standing upright or otherwise coming out of the goalie crouch. You must maintain a ready position—even, and especially, when moving, as it always opens more shooting opportunities for the offense.

The lateral glide, or T-glide, is used by the goalie when moving from post to post, quickly and under control.

Saves

Stick Save

Overview

The most basic save is the stick save. It is used to protect the space left open between the goaltender's two leg pads.

Technique (Freezing Puck)

1. Soft grip.

2. Remember, hold stick with the index finger and thumb just above the wide portion of the stick, where the blade and shaft meet. Wrap the three remaining fingers around shaft.

A goalie must always try to freeze the puck/ball in order to prevent rebounds, which allow additional shooting opportunities.

3. Hold stick out in front of your skates to provide a cushion space for when the puck comes in contact with the blade. This helps to cut down on rebounds.

4. Tilt stick blade slightly downward. Rest blade on surface.

5. Move stick from toe to toe in a rainbowlike, arcing motion.

6. Allow the stick to "give" when the shot puck strikes the blade.

Common Errors

- Stick blade is against toes of skates.

- Not cushioning the puck.

Directing the Rebound

Technique

1. Firm grip.

2. Stick blade held rigid against toes of skates.

3. Stick blade is upright; blade's heel is resting on the surface.

Common Error

- Allowing the blade to "give." Cushioning the puck is not appropriate when directing a rebound.

- Direct puck into the corners or to the sideboards when an opponent is looking for a rebound.

- One of the few, if not the only, instances when cushioning the puck is *not* called for.

Glove Save

Overview

The glove save is one of the most effective saves used by a goaltender. It is also unique because the glove save both stops and freezes the puck in one step. And since nearly everyone has caught a ball with a baseball/softball glove at some point, the glove save is familiar and relatively easy to learn.

The glove save is one of the most effective saves a goalie can use, since it stops and freezes the puck/ball in one step.

- The glove side is the goalie's strongest. A good shooter will try to avoid that side.
- A quick glove can cover nearly half of the net.
- Practice both forehand and backhand techniques.
- Open the glove as wide as possible so it takes up more space (i.e., reduces the shooting angle) in the net.

- By adding force and moving the blocker toward the approaching puck, the goaltender can rebound the puck with direction and accuracy. Direct puck away from flow of "traffic."
- Due to the weight of stick and blocker, the goaltender has limited vertical arm movement. A good shooter will position shots high to the stick side—one of the most vulnerable areas for the goaltender.

Technique

1. Glove is open, out, and in front of the body.

2. Watch puck all the way into glove.

3. Move glove in a pivoting action—up and down—as though it were a bird's wing.

4. Move body behind shot, if possible, in case puck gets by glove.

Common Errors

- Glove closed.

- Glove height too low—especially common among tired goaltenders.

- Moving the body toward the puck.

- Not watching the puck into the glove.

Blocker ("Stick Mitt," "Waffle") Save

Overview

The blocker save is used to stop a puck shot high on the goaltender's stick side. This save can be used either to direct a rebound or to freeze the puck by using the catch glove to trap the puck against the blocker.

Freezing the puck/ball with the blocker save

Technique

1. Move the blocker toward the direction of the shot.

2. Watch puck all the way to the blocker.

3. In one motion, move the catch glove to trap and freeze the puck against the blocker.

When using the blocker save the goalie should try to freeze the puck by using the glove hand.

4. Alternatively, angle (or tilt) the blocker to direct a rebound.

Common Errors

• Twisting the blocker around and exposing the fingers and palm to the shot. (If struck, these areas can be injured.)

• Taking eye off puck at last moment.

Body Save

Overview

The body save uses the goaltender's entire body—not a specific body part or piece of equipment—to stop the puck. This save requires no finesse, just an ability and confidence to place the body in front of a speeding puck. To have confidence in this technique, the goaltender must have no doubt that the protective equipment worn under his uniform is going to perform without fail.

Technique

1. Move body in front of the shot puck.

2. Use any part of the body to stop the puck.

Skate Save

Overview

The skate save is used both while standing and when out of position to stop a puck that is an inch or so above the playing surface. It is made with the wheels of the skate.

The skate save is made with the wheels of the skate.

Technique

1. Start from a basic goalie crouch position, low and knees bent.

2. Turn "save" skate 90 degrees toward either goalpost.

3. While gliding skate in an arcing motion toward the post, bring the knee of your trailing leg to the playing surface.

Coaches should always double-check the goalie's body armor. It takes only one 70-mph shot into an unprotected area of the body to make a once fearless goalie forever gun shy.

• When puck is shot at mid-chest height, goaltender may become "hand-cuffed"—that is, unsure whether to use the glove, blocker, or stick. This is a good situation to use the chest to stop the puck, then quickly trap and freeze puck with catch glove.

• This is a save of last resort. Try it when no other save technique can be used.

When you are in the final skate save position, an enormous gap is left between your legs. You should commit to this save only when you are sure the shooter has committed to shooting in this area. Watch for a deke (or fake) to force you to commit to a vulnerable saving position.

Follow the puck with your eyes all the way.

4. Position blocker or glove (depending on the side) slightly above "save" skate in case the puck is shot high or skips above the skate.

Common Errors

• At maximum extension, the toe of your "save" skate will tend to come up. Try to avoid this, instead keeping all the wheels on the surface.

• Coming up out of stance when moving toward save position.

• Leaning back, away from the shot. Keep weight slightly forward.

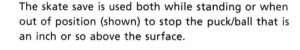

The skate save is used both while standing or when out of position (shown) to stop the puck/ball that is an inch or so above the surface.

Leg (Pad) Save

Overview

The leg (pad) save is used to stop low, hard shots. Because of their size, the leg pads stop upward of 60 percent of all shots on goal.

Technique

1. Keep face of pads facing the shooter as much as possible.

2. When moving laterally, do so quickly, since this turns the face of the glide leg pad to the side and exposes the unprotected leg.

The goalie guarding the post

Common Errors

• Wide gaps between each leg pad.

• Not watching puck all the way.

• Allowing puck to rebound (or deflect) back into play.

- When moving laterally, drive hard off the back wheel edge to reduce the amount of time that pads are not "square" to play.
- Practice moving laterally to both sides. Strengthen your weaker side so you are quick and smooth in either direction.
- Cushion shot by straightening your knees. This will help to prevent rebounds.
- Trap the puck with glove hand to freeze it.

Drop to V position, with your body in line with the puck. If the shot is high, your body will be in position to block it.

Butterfly, or V-Drop, Save

Overview

The butterfly (or V-drop) save is used as a last resort. This save is used generally when the puck is close in to the net.

Technique

1. Move out in front of crease.

2. Drop to inside of knees and lower legs. At the same time, the legs fan out.

3. With knees together, feet should fan outward, with toes pointing toward either goalpost, forming a V shape.

Butterfly save

4. Keep pads flush on the surface.

5. Keep stick blade centered between pads to protect the gap.

Common Error

- Gap between leg pads and the surface. Puck can slide through this gap and into the goal.

Two-Pad, or Stacking Pad, Save

Overview

The two-pad (or stacking-pad) save is used as a last resort. This save is used when the puck is shot close to the net.

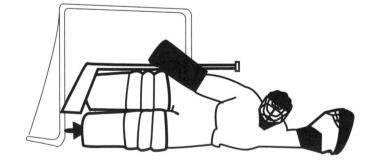

Two-pad save (glove side)

- Think of forming a wall. Use the top arm to increase the "wall's" height.
- Use the bottom arm to increase the length of the "wall."

Technique

1. Move to the right (or left).

2. Kick out both legs as though you were sliding into a base in baseball.

3. Stack the leg pads, or place one leg on top of the other, thus forming a "wall" to block the shot. The top arm should rest on top of your legs.

4. The bottom arm should remain flush to the surface. Be ready to swing your stick (or, from the other direction, your mitt) to stop a shot.

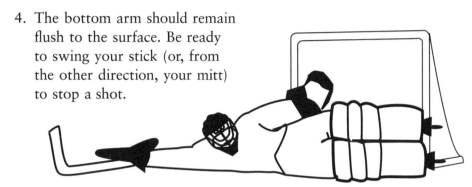

Two-pad save (stick side)

Common Errors

- Legs are not stacked evenly, one directly atop the other. Imagine you are laying one brick flush and even over another.

- Gap between surface and outstretched bottom arm, through which the puck may slip.

Cutting Down Shooting Angle

Overview

Proper positioning—being in the right place for each situation—is a significant factor in a goalkeeper's effectiveness. A good goaltender knows the importance of positioning to reduce the amount of open net.

With the help of curved stick blades and refinements in technique, players are learning to shoot harder, quicker, and from

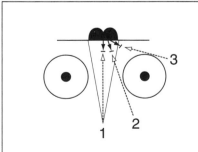

The goalie must move out from the goal in order to cut down the shooting angle. (The numerals represent three different shooting angles.)

- Practice skating out from the crease about five feet. Then move backward. *Do not* turn around and skate back to the crease forward. *Never* turn your back on a play.
- Practice moving out at different angles.
- Know where you are relative to the goal at all times. Use different marks on the rink surface as reference points.
- Practice. Practice. Practice.

- Imagine throwing an elbow at the puck.
- Make sure you have a knob on the end of your stick's shaft so the stick will not slide through your hand.
- Try combining the poke check with moving out from the goal crease to reduce the shooting angle.

farther out than ever before. This requires the goalie to play farther out in front of the goal to reduce the shooting angle.

As a goalie moves out from the goal, there is less net for the advancing opponent to see—and shoot at. But there is a flip side. By coming out from the goal, the goaltender gives the shooter more area to maneuver and get an angle on the goal. And since the goalie is weighted down with protective gear, he is no match for the relatively nimble attacker.

The goalie cutting down the shooting angle

Poke Check

Overview

Stopping shots from within the slot, the area directly in front of the goal crease, is difficult. Even a goaltender with the quickest of reflexes is unable to stop most shots on goal made from the slot. So, it is always preferable to prevent such a shot from being made in the first place. The poke check can be a very effective method of preventing these shots.

Technique

1. Stick hand is held close to body.

2. Elbow is bent.

3. Quickly extend arm and stick toward the puck. Use the full length of the shaft up to the knob.

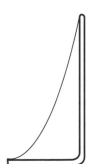

Goalie poke check

Common Errors

- Checking arm starts from an extended position.

- Lunging at the puck. This puts you out of balance.

Goaltending Situations
Controlling Rebounds

Overview

Use the stick blade as you recover to the goalie crouch. Just because you are on your knees does not mean you cannot be effective. Use your stick, gloves, pads, body—anything—to stop that puck.

It is not enough to just save shots. Since most goals are scored on rebounds and tips-ins (a deflected shot), the goalie must eliminate additional shooting opportunities by controlling rebounds in front of the net after successful saves.

Technique

1. Cushion the puck. This means "giving" with the stick on stick saves as well as with the leg pads on standing leg saves.

2. Smother, or "freeze," shots that cannot be redirected away from the opponents.

3. After each save, recover to the goalie crouch as quickly as possible. Think "Save and recover, save and recover."

Bouncing Puck

Overview

This situation applies more to games played with a true puck than a ball. Since a ball has no edges, it will usually bounce consistently and predictably.

A bouncing puck is similar to a baseball that takes a bad hop. This is one of the most difficult situations for a goalie to play. If the puck lands on its edge, it is virtually impossible to predict its direction.

Technique

1. Move out of the crease to meet the puck.

2. Square your body against the puck's angle of approach.

3. Use your entire body to block the puck and then smother it.

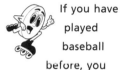

Goaltending is an ongoing process of "desperation," and this is what makes the position so exciting. Goalies are martyrs. Despite being shot at when you are down, you keep getting back up for more.

If you have played baseball before, you know that the best way to play a ground ball is to "square" your body to it. If it takes a bad hop, you can knock it down in front of you and complete the play.

Breakaway

Overview

A breakaway is a one-on-one situation—a goalie and an attacking opponent. There are no other forwards or defensive players from either team accompanying the opponent or defending the goal. Goalies hate breakaways because they usually lose the duel. Stopping a breakaway requires considerable talent and sometimes quite a bit of luck.

Technique

1. Move out from the net about 15 feet to meet the attacking opponent.

2. As the opponent approaches, skate back (facing the attacker) toward the net.

3. When the opponent makes a move, use whatever method you can to stop the initial shot. (Your teammates should be fast approaching to handle possible rebounds.)

Common Errors

- Do not commit in either direction until the attacker commits. Force the opponent to make the first move.

- Do not telegraph your intentions. Once the attacker knows what you plan to do, he has the advantage.

Defending the post when the puck/ball is behind the goal. This is one of the few times a goalie's head is seen looking behind the goal.

General Tips and Suggestions for Goalies

- Always keep your eye on the puck—even when it is at the opposite end of the rink.

- Play the puck, not the shooter's body position.

- Watch for an opponent telegraphing a shot by dropping the head or eyes. This is a clue to move out to block the shot. Anticipate, but do not commit until the shot is off.

- When playing outdoors, check the goal crease frequently for pebbles or other debris that may cause the puck to take a wild hop.

- If your vision is blocked because of player movement or strategic screens, lower your crouch to keep the puck in sight.

- Improve hand-eye coordination by playing ball sports such as racquetball, tennis, even Ping-Pong. And try this: In full gear, stand a few feet in front of a wall. Have a teammate, from about 20 feet away, throw a ball to different spots on the wall. See how quickly you can react. Try slapping the ball away, not letting it hit the wall behind you.

- Stretching is especially important for goaltenders. Since tending goal requires quick movements and extreme positions (leg kicks, V-drops, etc.), you can pull or strain a muscle easily if you are not limber.

CHAPTER 7

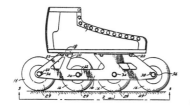 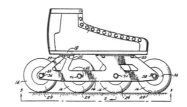 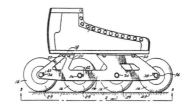

THE NIHA

What Is the NIHA?

The National In-line Hockey Association, or NIHA, is an independent organization that focuses on the development and promotion of amateur in-line roller hockey throughout North America and, increasingly, the world.

Founded in January 1993, the NIHA has structured itself progressively by placing its most important asset—indeed, its very reason for being—on the top of its organizational pyramid. And who would that be? You, of course—the in-line roller hockey player, coach, league manager, and referee.

NIHA-Provided Insurance

Liability. This is a frightening word in the world of amateur and recreational athletics, and no amount of protective gear, training, or contingency planning can eliminate the risk of personal injury. So we are left with *managing* the risk of personal injury and disaster—in a word, insurance.

The NIHA offers an insurance program tailored to fit the needs of almost any in-line roller hockey league. The program offers the following coverage:

Types of Coverage

- Member accident insurance
- Annual, daily
- Skate rental
- League general liability
- Hockey instructors
- Fire liability

What Is Covered?

- League play
- Tournament events
- Sites and venues
- Clinics and schools

Who Is Covered?

- Players
- Students
- Leagues
- Referees
- Coaches

- Instructors
- Landlords
- Retail stores
- Sponsors

Structure of the NIHA

The NIHA is committed to a "player first" philosophy. To get closer to its "rank and file," if you will, the NIHA has established an ever-expanding network of field lieutenants who help organize and assist in-line roller hockey leagues on a grassroots level.

Players

With a variety of membership programs, the NIHA has a level of in-line roller hockey suited to your abilities and preferences.

Team Captains

Team captains are selected by each team. Depending on the level of play, they have varying responsibilities. On adult teams, the captain takes the role of both team representative and team communicator, the coach's surrogate in contacting teammates and coordinating practices. On the youth level (ages 10 to 17), team captains serve similar functions, but with reduced responsibilities.

Coaches

Coaches, of course, have a tremendous responsibility for the safety and well-being of their players. They are part surrogate parent, part mentor, part friend. In addition to a thorough understanding of the game and its techniques, a coach must have a sound grounding in the psychology of coaching, basic first aid, safety, and organization.

Coaches' Conduct Code*

- Provide a safe play situation for your players.
- Treat each player as an individual.

---

*Adapted from "Coaches' Code of Ethics," National Youth Sport Coaches Association.

- Make practices fun and rewarding to players.

- Use coaching techniques that are appropriate to the skill level.

- Lead by example. Demonstrate fair play and proper conduct to all players.

- Know the rules of the game and communicate them effectively to your players.

- Remember to place the emotional and physical well-being of your players above any personal desire to win.

Referee signaling "holding" against a player.

Referees

Being a good, consistent referee takes more than just blowing a whistle and waving an arm. To be effective and respected, a referee must be a very good skater, have a keen sense of awareness, and exercise utmost restraint.

With the recent explosive growth of organized in-line roller hockey, the need for trained, competent officials has never been greater. The NIHA offers two different levels of referee certification training, each followed by a formal certification examination. Each of the one-day programs includes classroom work, utilizing a situations manual, and on-surface training in officiating techniques, including skating and proper positioning; rules and composure; calling/announcing of penalties; face-offs; and so forth.

Referees' Conduct Code*

- Know the rules, their interpretations, and their proper application.

- Be fair and impartial at all times.

- Be confident and decisive. Try for a commanding presence, but do not display arrogance.

- Do not tolerate violence or abusive language. Be strict and uncompromising.

- Do not openly criticize a coach, player, or other official.

- Stay calm and composed.

- Maintain your health, physique, and appearance.

- Be a good role model for players, coaches, and other officials.

NIHA Preferred Retailer Program

The NIHA's public service campaign takes a proactive approach by encouraging young people in high school and college to have fun by playing safely and responsibly.

The NIHA Preferred Retailer Program is an associate membership designed to expand and promote sales of in-line roller hockey equipment at participating specialty retailers. The NIHA directs queries about equipment to a preferred retailer in the community from which the query came.

In effect, these retailers become "local clubhouses" for in-line roller hockey by supporting the customers (i.e., in-line roller hockey players) that support them. Upon registration retailers receive a starter kit, including an information manual to educate employees and customers, NIHA point-of-purchase materials, as well as product discounts and distribution opportunities. Other benefits include skate-rental insurance coverage and event/tournament promotion assistance through the NIHA state league database.

*Developed by the National In-Line Hockey Association.

NIHA Alliances and Affiliations

Roller Skating Associations (RSA)

Roller Skating Associations is an expansive network of rink operators, roller/in-line skate manufacturers, instructors, and proficiency judges. Since 1937 the RSA has grown into an organizational powerhouse in the skating world by helping various trade organizations help themselves. The list of participating organizations is impressive; it includes the following: Roller Skating Rink Operators Association, Roller Skating Manufacturers, Society of Roller Skating Teachers of America, Speed Coaches Association, Roller Hockey Coaches Association, and Proficiency Judges.

In 1994, the National In-line Hockey Association entered an agreement with Roller Skating Associations to provide roller rink operators with both NIHA membership and participation in the Preferred Retailer program. In return, the RSA network of indoor roller rinks allows in-line roller hockey to be played year-round—even in the frigid winter climates of the Northeast, Midwest, and much of Canada.

United States Amateur Confederation of Roller Skating (USAC/RS)

Founded in 1937 as a part of the Roller Skating Rink Operators Association, the United States Amateur Confederation of Roller Skating (USAC/RS) is recognized as the official national governing body of all roller sports in the United States. Originally based in Detroit, Michigan, the Confederation moved to its present location— Lincoln, Nebraska—in 1968.

In 1994, the USAC/RS formally recognized the NIHA as an organizational body of in-line roller hockey. The two associations further agreed that there will be a free and reciprocal flow of players between organizations; that the "NIHA Official Rule Book" shall be consistent with the "fair play" principles of the national governing body; and that they will jointly develop in-line roller hockey players for world competition under international rules.

USAC/RS Mission*

- Over 25,000 members and more than 1,600 skating clubs across the country compete in three skating disciplines: artistic, speed, and (in-line) roller hockey.

- Maintains and updates athlete information and records.

- Provides training and educational opportunities for athletes and coaches.

- Handles travel arrangements for domestic and international outings.

- Selects Team USA for each of the three skating disciplines and sends each team to international competitions. (In 1992, the United States National Roller Hockey team was sent to play in the Barcelona Summer Olympics.)

- Sets and enforces competitive rules of play. Determines competitive divisions.

- Promotes roller skating and its athletes at home and abroad.

NIHA-Sanctioned Leagues

Adult League

The Adult League is designed for individuals 18 years and older who are involved in an organized in-line hockey league.

---

* "Backgrounder," United States Amateur Confederation of Roller Skating, 1992.

Youth League

The Youth League is the largest category of in-line hockey players by far. This program is subdivided into four age groups to ensure a close match of strength and abilities between competing teams. The age groups are 16–17; 13–15; 12–13; and 10–11.

(Parents): In-line roller hockey is *not* an alternative form of day care designed to get your kids out of your hair for a few hours a week. Quite the contrary. This game and your child's involvement in it require your own time and commitment. But although the game is for your child first and foremost, you may well find your role rewarding on a very personal level.

Parental Involvement and Support

Involvement with and support of your sons and daughters in their respective leagues can make the sport a fun-filled experience for them instead of one that is resented.

Parental Commandments

Be supportive and involved.
Help your coach and league officials provide the finest in-line hockey program they can. Volunteer time and resources whenever possible. Organize car pools with other parents or guardians.

Be positive.
Encourage good sportsmanship by demonstrating a positive attitude. Place the emotional and physical well-being of your child ahead of the desire to win.

Be committed.
Stand behind your child by assuring that he is properly outfitted for the game. *Do not* cut corners on equipment. *Do not* purchase oversized equipment to allow for your child's growth; this jeopardizes your child's safety. *Do* attend games and practices. Cheer your child and team on.

Be a role model.
Don't second-guess the coach, referee, or team officials from the bench. If you want to be a coach or a referee, be one—but not from the bleachers! Insist upon a drug-, smoke-, and alcohol-free environment for your child. Insist that your child treat others (players, coaches, fans, and officials) with respect and dignity at all times.

NIHA Instruction and Clinics

In-line Roller Hockey School (Players)

NIHA members receive a special discount off registration fees.

Like most team sports, in-line roller hockey requires a certain amount of practice and instruction. And while books and instructional videos may be helpful, nothing can replace a qualified coach or instructor.

Huron Hockey School, the official instructional program of the NIHA, is dedicated to improving each player's personal skill development. Huron is founded on the philosophy that hockey is best taught by people who have a qualified background in both hockey *and* education.

The school's instructional programs focus on fundamental skating techniques by using videotape analysis. In addition to on-surface instruction, students participate in "controlled" scrimmages and workshops, view instructional videos, and attend lectures.

Huron Hockey School offers four programs, each with specific areas of emphasis:

1. Minor Development. Designed for the young, developing player (ages 7 to 9). Areas of emphasis include balance and blade control, skating power and efficiency, and most important of all, hockey for the fun of it.

Clinics are most effective when operated on weekends—when sports-related buying is at its highest. Not only do such clinics generate sales for the retailer, but they also encourage fun and friendship within the local community.

2. Advanced Progressive. Designed for older, more developed players (ages 10 to 13). Areas of emphasis include acceleration, agility and speed, positional play, and game situations.

3. High School. Designed for the high-school-level player in various age and skill categories (ages 13 to 19). Areas of emphasis include advanced skill instruction, tricks of the trade, and offensive and defensive concepts.

4. Specialized Goaltender. Designed for a variety of age groups and skill levels (ages 7 to 19). Areas of emphasis include fundamental goal-saving development (or advanced skill development) and "showdown" and skills competition.

In-line Roller Hockey Clinics (Players)

In-line roller hockey clinics are a great introduction to the game. Since an in-line roller hockey rink can be set up in a parking lot, many NIHA preferred retailers are well situated (and equipped) to operate these demonstrations. These clinics are also a perfect instrument to test whether or not a community is right (or ready) for in-line roller hockey.

How to Start a League

You have just finished playing a pickup game of in-line roller hockey, and you had a blast. You have heard that this is a fast-growing sport, but in your community in-line skating is just now becoming popular, and organized in-line roller hockey is not available at all.

You decide that you may like to organize the group you play with and form an in-line roller hockey league. You proceed to distribute some flyers around skate shops and sporting-goods stores, and the next thing you know, people are calling you. "I want to get involved," they say. You now know that there is a large group wanting to play in-line roller hockey, but you realize that you still have more questions than answers: What rules should be enforced? Where will we play? What equipment do we need? And what happens if someone gets hurt?

Welcome to the National In-line Hockey Association. The NIHA was founded, in large part, to help you with the business of starting a

NIHA League Membership Package

- Insurance coverage for you, your site, your sponsor, and your members

- Sanctioning documents for each site

- NIHA banner for your site/facility

- "Winning In-line Hockey" video

- Support and oversight by your own state/province league coordinator

- Administrative computer software to help you organize your rosters, schedules, statistics, and equipment

- Referee certification and examination materials

- Coaching certification assistance (i.e., "coach school")

- Sign-up sheet for preregistration

- Complimentary NIHA travel discount card for the league manager

- State/provincial, regional, and national championships

- Manufacturer sales representative liaison with member leagues

- Personalized membership registration forms

- Official NIHA game sheets

- Official rule book for you, your referees, coaches, and members

- Toll-free assistance: (800) 358-NIHA, (800) 668-NIHA in Canada

- Membership ID cards, personalized for each member

- Membership perks package containing manufacturer incentives and rebates. Value is always increasing as NIHA forms new alliances and affiliations.

league. With its network of field personnel, NIHA is positioned to provide the information, resources, and contacts you need to get your in-line roller hockey in line!

Step-by-Step League Formation Procedure

Step 1. Survey Your Local Market

If you are interested in the idea of starting an in-line hockey league in your area, it is important that you determine if (and where) people are already playing the game. One option is to survey the area, perhaps put on a clinic or exhibition, then start to develop a database.

The survey should help you do the following:

- Determine if in-line roller hockey is being played in your community.

- Determine costs to lease or purchase a rink facility.

- Determine operational costs (equipment, labor, etc.).

- Determine the number of games, practices, and playoff games (a guaranteed minimum) for each player.

- Determine the cost per player (arrived at by dividing your costs plus profits by the number of prospective players).

- Start a mailing list.

- Meet with your local in-line retailer(s).

- Investigate other sports program memberships to determine if they would like to play in-line roller hockey.

Step 2. Identify a Site for League Play

Thanks to the in-line skate itself and a lot of manufacturer support of the game with innovative products (mobile rink structures, pucks and

The Border Patrol rink boundary system is composed of 50 foam "boards" that are lightweight and easy to carry. Completely transportable, the rink system can be set up or taken down in about 15 minutes and fits nicely in a van or full-size pickup truck. The boards feature a wide base and a narrow top in order to stack them efficiently for storage and transportation.

balls, etc.), in-line roller hockey is accessible to virtually any community. Possible sites include: parking lots, tennis courts, basketball courts, indoor roller rinks, off-season ice rinks (i.e., with ice melted), vacant warehouse space, and an ever-increasing number of in-line hockey facility and sports centers.

Step 3. Determine Space Requirements

Compared with baseball or football, the space requirements for in-line roller hockey are modest indeed. The NIHA recommends that the dimensions of the rink be from 145 to 200 feet long and from 65 to 100 feet wide.

The next step is to determine what type of border system you will use for your rink. Check Appendix C for vendors of various border systems.

Step 4. Sanction and Insure Your League

- Obtain permission from the site landlord or owner.

- Complete the NIHA site-sanctioning documents.

Turn a parking lot or tennis court into an in-line roller hockey rink.

The Border Patrol rink system (pictured here) is easy to set up. The vinyl-wrapped, foam boards weigh seven pounds each.

Velcro straps make setup and breakdown of the rink easy.

To make your rink as safe as possible, always clean the surface of any gravel or debris.

- All surfaces must be deemed safe by the NIHA.

For your protection, following the proper sanctioning procedure is imperative. Fully completed sanctioning documents, along with the sanctioning fee, should be mailed to the NIHA prior to registering individual members.

Once your application is approved, a sanctioning package will be sent to you. The package includes a general liability policy and certificate, an instructional in-line hockey skills video, computer software to help with league administration, an NIHA banner, NIHA tournament game sheets, and NIHA registration forms.

Step 5. Develop a Budget and a Business Plan

Your expenses may include any of the following:

- NIHA site-sanctioning fee

- Referee fees

- Rink system rental/purchase

- Jerseys

- Equipment

- Goal nets

- Balls or pucks

- Goalie equipment (strongly recommended)

- Score clock

- Statistician/timekeeper fees

- Trophies

- Marketing and promotion material

- Sponsorship through your local retailer or merchants

- Dasher board advertising

- League dues per player/per team

The perks of play. The NIHA National Championship takes place each fall, usually in October.

Step 6. Preregistration Advertising Suggestions

- Posters

- League brochures listing registration dates

- Sign-up sheets in retail stores

- Parks and recreation newsletters

- School flyers (posted on bulletin boards)

- School newspapers

- School seminars/clinics to generate interest

- Local television, radio, and newspapers

Step 7. Organize a Player/Parent League Meeting

Schedule a meeting and meet with the league's players and their parents (or guardians) to explain the program. Where will you play? How will players get to practices and games? Are parents willing to carpool? When will the season begin? (If you live in a cold climate and do not have an indoor facility, this fact should enter into that decision.) How many games will there be and on what days and times will they take place? If you have enough players, you may need to bracket the teams by age groups to match skill development and strength levels. Will your league have play-offs at the end of the season? Are the players (or parents) able and willing to pay the expenses associated with traveling to regional and national competitions?

Where is your local in-line roller hockey retail store? Is it an NIHA preferred retailer? If so, it can assist in processing memberships, distribute member perk packages, and offer NIHA discounts on products and services.

Step 8. Coaching

Included in the NIHA League Administration Package is NIHA league administrative software, which allows a league manager to perform all bookkeeping, planning, scheduling, inventory, and record-keeping functions with efficiency and ease. Developed by Hove Martin of Canada.

Anyone with an interest in coaching a team should contact a community league manager (CLM). The CLM should then coordinate a coaching clinic with the National Youth Sports Coaching Association (NYSCA). (The NYSCA is the recognized coaching arm of the NIHA.)

Step 9. Refereeing

Referee Certification Clinics are organized by both the State League Coordinator and the NIHA headquarters for local referee clinics. Level 1 certification can be achieved by taking a written examination provided by the NIHA. A completed exam, a referee registration form, and fee should be sent to the NIHA. Upon successful completion of the training, the referee will receive a certificate of completion, an NIHA rule book, an NIHA certification card, and excess medical coverage.

Step 10. Registration

- Call on student interns and/or volunteer parents to help with administrative duties.
- Have an adequate supply of NIHA registration forms on hand and sufficient staffing.
- Complete all information clearly and completely.
- Forward all the registrations to the NIHA within 72 hours.
- Identify the length of the youth registration: three months, six months, or a full year.
- Allow four weeks for processing membership.

Locate a convenient, "high-traffic" location. Some ideas: a local hockey retail store, a park or recreation area, an in-line hockey arena. Inform all would-be players of fees, benefits, and requirements.

Courtesy of Jamie Itagaki

"Wanna play? So what are you waiting for?"

GLOSSARY

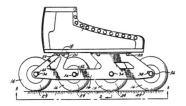 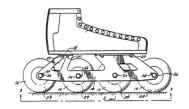 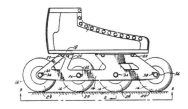

A

ABEC. Annular Bearing Engineering Council, the organization that developed the internationally recognized scale of bearing quality. In-line wheels are rated on the so-called Shore "A" ABEC scale: for example, ABEC 3.

AHAUS The Amateur Hockey Association of the United States. Name changed to *USA Hockey*.

Allen Wrench. A tool used for securing the wheel axle to the skate frame. Named after Joseph P. Allen.

Aluminum Shaft. A thick stick shaft made of foam-filled aluminum. The wooden blade is detachable from the shaft, making it easy to switch broken blades while keeping the

same flex and torsion in the shaft. This helps cut down on stick maintenance.

ANSI. American National Standards Institute, an organization that sets standards for protective equipment. ANSI standards are regarded as easier to meet than those of *Snell*.

ASTM. Founded in 1898, the American Society for Testing Materials is a not-for-profit organization that provides a forum for producers, users, ultimate consumers, and those having a general interest to meet and determine standards for materials, products, systems, and services. It is based in Philadelphia, Pennsylvania.

Athletic Protector. A padded piece of equipment designed to fit over and around the groin area of male players to protect against impact injury. Also referred to as a "cup."

Attack Zone. The area between the center line and the opponents' goal line for a team in possession of the puck.

Attempt to Injure. An action by a player or team official who attempts to hit an opposing player, team official, or game official with the intent to cause injury.

B

Back-Check. Checking action taken by the forward line or defense of a team in their own defensive zone against opposing forwards.

Backhand Pass. A pass made with the back portion of the stick's blade.

Backhand Shot. A shot that is like the backhand pass but more forceful.

Bearing. An encasement containing ball bearings that is often shielded and prepacked in grease.

Blind Pass. A pass made without looking where the puck will wind up.

Blocker Mitt. A large, leather-covered, rectangular piece of thick plastic attached to the back of a leather glove and worn on a goalkeeper's stick-holding hand. Also known as *stick mitt* or *waffle mitt.*

Blocker Save. An attempt by the goalkeeper to stop a shot puck with the blocker mitt.

Board the Puck. To hit the puck against the sideboards.

Boards. The walls or other boundaries that surround the playing surface.

Body Check. See *Checking.*

Body Save. A save made by a goalkeeper with any part of the body.

Breakaway. A game situation in which a player has full control of the puck and there is no opposing skater between himself and the opposing goal.

Breakout. A game situation that occurs whenever a team comes out of its defending zone with the puck and proceeds to go on the attack.

Butt End. See *Knob.*

Butt-Ending. Action of using the shaft of the stick above the upper hand to check, jab, or attempt to jab an opposing player in any manner.

C

C. The letter worn on the team captain's jersey.

Cantering. Adjusting the skate frame laterally to maximize skating stride. By moving the front frame mounting inward, the wheel angle changes, thereby maximizing the skating stride.

Captain. A player, other than a goalkeeper, who is selected to represent the team in dealing with officials.

Carom. A rebound of the puck off the sideboards or any other surface.

Catching Glove. See *Catching Mitt.*

Catching Mitt. This piece of equipment, which resembles a first baseman's mitt in baseball, is used by a goalkeeper to catch a puck in flight. Also known as a *glove mitt* or *catching glove.*

Center of Gravity. The area of the body that is evenly balanced and distributed, and the point on which gravity acts. It is crucial that you maintain your center of gravity to prevent falling.

Charging. The act of taking more than two steps or strides to make contact with an opposing player. Illegal under NIHA rules of play.

Checking. Use of the body to hit a puck carrier in a pushing, shoving, or knocking action in an attempt to make the puck carrier lose control of the puck. Illegal under NIHA rules of play.

Clearing the Puck. Getting the puck out of the zone being defended.

CLM. Community league manager. An NIHA representative responsible for promoting and administering in-line roller hockey league activity on a local level.

Coach. A person responsible for directing the actions of his team. He is responsible for the conduct of the players before, during, and after the game in the playing area.

Core. The center portion of a skate wheel. It comprises the hub, bearings, spacers, and axle.

Cover. A defensive player guarding an opponent closely in his own defensive end so that the opponent cannot receive a pass.

Cradling. Nestling the puck inside the curve of the stick to protect it from opponents and to move it about the playing surface.

Crashing the Net. The act of one or more members of an attacking team who skate directly toward the opponents' net to overflow the offensive zone and thus confuse the defense.

Crease. The semicircular area directly in front of the net. It is 6 feet from the midpoint of the goal line.

Cross-Checking. Using the shaft of the stick between the two hands to check an opponent at any height. Illegal under NIHA rules of play.

Crossover. A turn in which the outside skate is lifted off the skating surface, crossed over the inner skate, and planted on the other side of the inside skate.

Cross-Surface Pass. A pass made between two teammates that crosses, untouched, over the center passing lane.

Cross-Training. Using one sport's conditioning benefits to improve performance in another sport.

CSA. Canadian Safety Association. The Canadian counterpart to *HECC*, this organization tests and certifies protective hockey equipment.

Cupping. The act of closing one's hand on the puck.

D

Defense Players. The two skaters on the playing surface directly in front of the goalkeeper who help to prevent the puck from entering the net.

Deflection. The redirection of the puck from its original glide path toward the goal by a stick, leg, skate, or other means.

Deke. A fake by a puck carrier in the opposite direction of his intended route. Short for "decoy."

Delayed Whistle. When a violation occurs, the official will not blow the whistle to stop play as long as the nonoffending team has possession of the puck. The moment the offending team touches the puck, play is stopped.

Delaying the Game. A penalty called against a team for causing unnecessary stoppages of play.

Diameter. The size of a skate wheel, measured in millimeters.

Digging. Working hard for possession of the puck, such as along the boards.

Dragging. Placing a skate at a right angle to the forward motion. A skater can use this technique to slow himself down.

Draw. See *Face-Off.*

Dribble. To move the puck from side to side or back and forth with the blade of the stick.

Drop Pass. The action of leaving the puck behind on the playing surface for a trailing teammate to pick up.

Durometer. A measure of the hardness of a skate wheel. Also, the tool used to make this measurement.

E

Elbowing. Hitting an opponent with your elbow. Illegal under NIHA rules of play.

Empty Net. A game situation in which there is no player guarding the net.

F

Face. The front side of a hockey stick blade.

Face Mask. A coated wire cage or plastic shield, worn by goalkeepers and non-adult players, that completely covers the face from the eyes to the lip area. Must be approved by HECC or CSA.

Face-Off. Action of the referee dropping the puck between the sticks of two opposing players to start or resume play. A face-off officially begins when the referee indicates where the puck will be dropped and ends when the puck has been properly dropped. Also called *draw.*

Face-Off Circle. Any of the five areas on the surface in which most face-offs occur.

Fast Start. An explosive skating start that gives a player a quick jump into the play.

Feather. To handle the puck gently and lightly with the stick blade.

Feeding. Passing the puck to a teammate.

FIRS. Federation Internationale de Roller Skating. Roller-skating's international governing body, and a member of the International Olympic Committee (IOC).

Five Hole. On a goalkeeper in a normal goalie crouch, the area between the leg pads just below the crotch and above the stick blade. This is a vulnerable area, since it is very difficult for a goalie to defend against a puck's being shot through it.

Flip Backhand Shot. A backhand shot in which the puck is flipped into the air to pass it over an obstacle.

Flip Pass. A short, quick pass to a teammate executed by a flip of the wrist to get the puck just off the surface and over any low obstructions—skates, for instance.

Floater. An offensive player who slips behind an attacking defense player looking for a breakaway. Also called "sleeper" and "hanger."

Follow-Through. The process of moving the stick up and through the path of the puck after the puck is shot.

Forehand Pass. A pass of the puck made with the hands in the usual positions on the stick, and the puck inside the curve of the blade.

Forward. Either of the two players who make up a line that leads a team into its attack zone and initiates most of the scoring opportunities.

Freezing the Puck. Preventing the puck from moving in any direction by holding or otherwise stopping it. When the puck is frozen, the referee will blow his whistle to stop play.

Full Strength. A game situation in which a team plays with all its skaters—that is, no player is serving a minor or major penalty.

G

Game. A meeting of two teams who play each other for a specific length of time, for the purpose of declaring a winner through the scoring of goals.

Game Disqualification. When a player has been ejected from the game, this player must leave the area of the players' bench and must in no way direct, coach, or assist the team in any manner for the remainder of the game.

Game Misconduct. A penalty assessed to a player or team official for committing an infraction of the rules that calls for automatic suspension.

Garbage Goal. A goal scored from a scramble in front of the net, or a lucky goal.

Get a Shot Off. Shooting the puck toward the goal.

Give-and-Go. A maneuver in which the puck is passed to a teammate and the passer moves immediately in the direction of the goal in anticipation of a return pass.

Glove Mitt. See *Catching Mitt.*

Glove Save. The action by the goalkeeper of stopping the puck from going into the net by using the catching mitt.

Goal Mouth. The space formed by the goalposts and crossbar. It measures 6 feet by 4 feet.

Goalie. See *Goaltender.*

Goalkeeper. See *Goaltender.*

Goaltender. The player charged with the responsibility of preventing the puck from going into the net. Also called *goalie, goalkeeper, keep,* or *netminder.*

Gross Misconduct. A penalty category that calls for the offending player or team official to be excluded from play for the remainder of the game. Another player is permitted to replace the penalized player.

Hard Pass. A pass made with considerable force and velocity.

Hat Trick. Three goals by a single player in one game.

Head-Man Pass. A quick lead pass by a player to a center or wing breaking into the center zone.

HECC. Hockey Equipment Certification Committee. Tests and certifies goal hockey equipment. See *CSA.*

Heel of the Stick. The point where the shaft of the stick and the bottom of the blade meet.

High-Sticking. The action of a player who carries the stick above the normal height of the waist.

Hockey Gloves. Special, highly protective gloves that a skater uses to hold the stick. Unlike other gloves, the fingers are not flexible; they do not wrap around the stick shaft, but hold it clawlike.

Holding. Any act of physical restraint by a player that impedes the motion of an opposing player.

Hooking. Using the blade of a stick in a pulling or tugging motion to impede the progress of an opponent.

Hub. The center of a skate wheel, including the core, bearings, and spacers.

I

IISA. International In-line Skating Association. Founded in July 1991, reorganized in January 1993. The national trade organization for in-line skating activities, the association develops safety and education programs, and works to protect and expand access to all in-line skating activities. Originally an outgrowth of the RSA, IISA is based in Atlanta, Georgia.

Insoles. The inner lining of footwear on which the foot rests.

Interference. The action of a player who interferes with or impedes the progress of an opponent who is not in possession of the puck. Illegal under NIHA rules of play.

IOC. International Olympic Committee.

ISA. International Skating Association.

K

Keep. See *Goalkeeper*.

Kick Save. A save by the goalkeeper that involves kicking the leg pad toward the puck.

Kicked Goal. A goal made by kicking the puck into the opponent's net intentionally. A puck may be propelled on the surface by kicking the puck, but a goal may not be scored in this way.

Kicking. Action of a player who, with no intent to play the puck, deliberately uses his skate(s) to contact an opponent.

Killing a Penalty. Preventing another team from scoring on a power play.

Knob. The top of the stick's shaft. Also known as the *butt end*.

L

Lead Pass. A pass to a teammate who is ahead of the puck carrier.

Leading. Anticipating the receiving skater's location when making a pass, so the receiver does not have to break stride or slow down in order to gain control of the puck.

Leading the Receiver. Passing to a point at which the puck and the receiver will meet.

Left-Handed Shot. A shot that is made with both the puck and the stick on the left side of the shooter's body.

Leg Pads. Thick, heavy pads worn by the goalkeeper on the legs. Used for protection and to stop the puck.

Lie. The angle formed by a hockey stick's shaft and blade.

Lift Pass. A pass made in such a way that the puck leaves the surface to pass over an obstruction.

Loose Puck. A puck that is not being controlled by any player while the game is in progress.

M

Major Infraction. See *Major Penalty*.

Major Penalty. A 5-minute penalty called for a major infraction.

Match. See *Game*.

Merlin, Joseph. First inventor of a roller skate to receive a patent. His patent was issued in 1863.

Minor Infraction. See *Minor Penalty*.

Minor Officials. Officials appointed to assist the on-surface officials (referees) in the conduct of the game. They include a scorer, game timekeeper, penalty timekeeper, and goal judges.

Minor Penalty. A 2-minute penalty called for a minor infraction.

Mireault, Joseph R. Founder and president of the National In-line Hockey Association (NIHA).

Misconduct Penalty. A penalty that calls for the removal of a player, other than a goalkeeper, for a period of 10 minutes. Another player is permitted to replace the penalized player.

Mondo Point. A worldwide sizing system established in 1990 by the International Standards Organization and later adopted by the American Society for Testing Materials (ASTM). Based on the length of the foot in centimeters.

N

National Governing Body. See *USAC/RS.*

Netminder. See *Goaltender.*

Neutral Zone. The center zone of the playing surface. Considered neither an attacking nor a defending area.

NHL. National Hockey League. Founded in 1917.

NIHA. National In-line Hockey Association. Founded in January 1993 to organize and promote amateur in-line roller-skating

throughout North America and, increasingly, the world. NIHA is based in Miami, Florida.

Nik/Niki. The official mascots of NIHA junior members, age 10 and under. "NIK" stands for "National In-line Kids."

NYSCA. The National Youth Sports Coaches Association. Founded in 1981 to help improve out-of-school training and the education of volunteer coaches, it is based in West Palm Beach, Florida.

O

Off Wing. The wing opposite the normal position a forward or wing plays.

Offsetting Penalties. A game situation in which a player from each team is penalized for infractions that occurred simultaneously. Usually assessed for roughing or fighting.

Offsides. A situation in which any offensive player precedes the puck into the offensive zone. The offsides rule is not observed under NIHA game rules.

Olson, Scott. Inventor of the Rollerblade in-line skate. Founded Rollerblade, Inc., in 1981.

On-Surface Official. See *Referee.*

Open Net. A goal that is not being guarded by the goalkeeper or any other player.

Open Player. A skater who is not being guarded by a member of the opposing team.

Open Surface. The part of the playing surface that is free of opponents.

Oxygen Debt. The state when your body is not delivering oxygen to your extremities fast enough, resulting in a feeling of sluggishness.

P

Pad Save. A save made by a goalkeeper with any part of the leg pad.

Pass. A transfer of control of the puck from one player to a teammate.

Passing Alley. A clear surface lane in which a pass can be made.

Pass-Out. A pass by an attacking player from behind the opponents' goal or from the corner to a teammate in front of the goal.

Penalty. Playing time served in the penalty box by a player for an infraction of the game rules.

Penalty Box. An isolated, off-surface area, usually located across from the players' bench, in which players serve penalty time.

Penalty Killers. Players who serve in a defensive role while their team is shorthanded due to a penalty.

Period. Either of the two equal time spans into which a game is divided. Under NIHA rules, the maximum time allowed for each period is 22 minutes.

Pinching. The act of a defense player who moves in from his point position to keep the puck in the attacking zone.

Play. A term used to describe a game in session when the official clock is keeping time.

Player Advantage. A game situation in which, because of a penalty, a team plays with an extra skater—that is, four against three.

Player Short. A team with one player in the penalty box, leaving the opposing team with one more player on the surface, is said to be a player short.

Players. Members of the teams physically participating in the game (except where special rules apply to an individual).

PLC. Provincial league coordinator. The Canadian counterpart to a U.S. state league coordinator (SLC).

Point. The normal position of a defensive player in his team's offensive zone: inside the blue line and near the sideboards.

Polyurethane. Any polymer that contains NHCOO (nitrogen, hydrogen, carbon, and oxygen) chemical linkages. This is the primary material used in the manufacture of in-line skate wheels.

Possession. Control of the puck.

Power Play. When a team is assessed a penalty and must play a player short, the opposing team is said to have a power play for the length of the penalty.

Power Slide. Derived from ice hockey, this is the most aggressive stop in in-line roller hockey. It is executed by turning and extending the lead skate at an angle against the surface, as if a thin layer were being shaved from the surface.

Profile. The profile of a wheel is the outline, or sidecut, of the rolling surface. It shows how much of the wheel is actually in contact with the skating surface.

Protective Equipment. Equipment worn by a player for the sole purpose of protecting against injury.

Puck. A spherical (ball) or circular (puck) piece of molded plastic usually orange in color, used in the game of in-line roller hockey.

Puck Out of Sight. A game situation where the puck cannot be seen by the referee, typically when a goalkeeper falls on it. The whistle is blown, play is stopped, and the puck is faced off.

Pure Shooter. A player who is considered to be expert in getting off shots and is usually a productive goal scorer.

Push Pass. A pass that advances the puck forward with a restrained shove rather than a full swing. Also called *Shovel Pass.*

R

Ragging. Retaining possession of the puck without the intention of scoring. This is a type of "keep-away."

Rebound. 1) The amount of energy that a wheel absorbs, then returns.

2) A puck that bounces/rolls back into play after a successful save by the goalkeeper.

Ref. See *Referee.*

Referee. An on-surface official supervising the play of a game. Also called *Ref.*

Referees' Crease. An area, marked by a line (often red), in front of the timer's table which a player is prohibited from entering while the referee is reporting a penalty.

RHI. Roller Hockey International. Founded in 1992.

Right-Handed Shot. A shot that is made with both the puck and the stick on the right side of the shooter's body.

Rink. The structure that defines the surface on which in-line roller hockey is played. The rink may range from 65 to 100 feet in width and 145 to 200 feet in length.

Rockering. Changing the height of two or more wheels by adjusting the position of the axle or the wheel size (diameter). This creates a curved wheel line relative to the skating surface. While this increases the skate's maneuverability, it does so at the expense of skating stability.

Rollerblading. A misnomer commonly used to refer to in-line skating. Rollerblade is a registered trademark, and any published use of the term to describe the activity is an infringement of trademark law. The correct terminology is "in-line skating," "in-line roller hockey," etc. Also incorrect: "blading," "blader," "blades," and so forth.

RSA. Roller Skating Associations. Founded in 1937, this is the national trade association of the roller-skating industry. It is made up of the Roller Skating Rink Operators

Association, the Roller Skating Manufacturers, the Society of Roller Skating Teachers of America, the Speed Coaches Association, the Roller Hockey Coaches Association, and the Proficiency Judges.

RSROA. Roller Skating Rink Operators Association. The original parent organization of the United States Amateur Confederation of Roller Skating.

Rush. An individual or combined attack by a team in possession of the puck toward the attacking zone.

S

Scooting. A skating motion, consisting of short thrusts, used in confined areas.

Scramble. A term used to describe the confusion that results when a number of players attempt to gain control of a loose puck.

Screen. A player who blocks the goalkeeper's view of the puck.

Shadowing. The act of closely guarding one specific player.

Shooting Angle. A shooter's position on the playing surface in relation to the goal mouth.

Shoot-Out. A one-on-one matchup between skaters and opposing goalies in which a skater takes the puck from the center face-off spot and moves toward the goalkeeper in an attempt to score a goal. A shoot-out is used to break ties in tournament or playoff games following an overtime period.

Shorthanded. A term used to describe a team playing with fewer skaters than its opponent.

Shot on Goal. A shot made in the direction of the goal.

Shovel Pass. See *Push Pass*.

Skate Save. A save made by a goalkeeper with the skate wheels or boot of the skate.

Slap Shot. A quick, hard shot made by drawing the stick back high above the shoulder, then pulling down and driving through the puck with full force and high follow-through to give the puck power and speed.

Slashing. Hitting, or attempting to hit, another player with a stick. A player found to be slashing will be penalized.

SLC. State league coordinator. An NIHA representative responsible for promoting and administering in-line roller hockey activity on a state level. The SLC's Canadian counterpart is the PLC, or provincial league coordinator.

Slide Shot. A shot that is like a push pass.

Slot. The area of the playing surface directly in front of the goal crease between the face-off circles. It is approximately 10 feet wide and 15 feet long.

Smother. A maneuver, usually by the goalkeeper, to stop the puck by falling on it.

Snap Pass. A quick pass made by moving the stick with a snap of the wrists.

Snap Shot. A shot similar to the slap shot but with the stick coming back only one half or one quarter the distance it does in the slap shot.

Snell. Refers to the Snell Memorial Foundation, an organization that, like ANSI, develops standards for protective equipment. Headquartered in St. James, New York, it is named after race car driver Pete Snell, who was killed in a car crash in the 1950s while wearing a helmet that was more decorative than functional. Snell certification stickers are green or blue and bear a serial number.

Solo. A rush by a player without the assistance of his teammates.

Spearing. Action of poking or attempting to poke an opponent with the toe/point of the stick blade with one or both hands. This is illegal under NIHA rules of play.

Split. The action of the goaltender when he goes down to the playing surface to make a kick save.

Split Vision. The ability to look straight ahead and yet see players on either side and the puck on one's stick.

Splitting the Defense. A puck carrier breaking through two defending players.

Spot Pass. A pass to a spot, rather than to a player, in the expectation that a teammate will arrive at the spot and receive the pass.

Stalling. Delaying the game—by, for example, intentionally shooting the puck over the boards. Illegal under NIHA rules of play.

Stand-Up Goalie. A goalkeeper who attempts to stop most shots while standing up, rather than by dropping to the ice.

Starts and Stops. A common skating drill.

Stick Blade. The wide, flat, sometimes curved wooden part of the stick at the bottom of the shaft. The puck is shot and passed with the stick blade.

Stick Lie. See *Lie*.

Stick Mitt. See *Blocker Mitt*.

Stick Save. A save made by the goalkeeper using the stick.

Stick Shaft. The handle of the stick, extending from the blade to the knob. Although often made of wood, it can also be made of hollow aluminum or a metal composite.

Support Strap. An additional skate buckle used to tighten the cuff (the top of the skate boot).

Sweep Check. A sweeping motion of a stick flat on the playing surface to take the puck away from an opponent.

T

Team Official. Coach, league manager, trainer, and so forth.

Telegraphing. Looking directly at a teammate before passing the puck, or signaling your intentions in any way.

Tip-In. Placing of the stick blade in the path of a puck, thus deflecting or redirecting it into the goal.

Toe Save. A save made by a goalkeeper with the tip of an outstretched skate.

Trailing. The act of following a play, without being directly involved in the play.

U

USA Hockey. The governing body of amateur ice hockey. Formerly *AHAUS*.

USAC/RS. United States Amateur Confederation of Roller Skating. Founded in 1937 as part of the *RSROA*. The national governing body for all roller-skating activities.

USOC. United States Olympic Committee.

W

Waffle Mitt. See *Blocker Mitt*.

Warm-Up. A session prior to the start of a game during which the players stretch and help the goalkeeper prepare for the game.

Wooden Shaft. A stick made of wood. The wooden shaft is permanently attached to the stick blade.

Wraparound. 1) A hard shot made into the attack zone along the boards. The momentum of the shot wraps the puck around and behind the goal and into the opposite corner, where it is met by another player. 2) An attempt to score by coming out from behind the goal and sweeping the puck into the net.

WRHL. World Roller Hockey League. Merged with Roller Hockey International (RHI) in 1993.

Wrist Shot. A quick shot using wrist strength to snap the puck.

Z

Zero Tolerance. An in-line hockey rule forbidding the use of profane language.

Zone. Any of three areas on the playing surface: the attack zone, the neutral zone, and the defensive zone.

Zone Clear. Shooting the puck from one end of the surface to the other in an effort to get it out of the zone quickly. If the puck crosses the goal line, it is a violation, and a face-off will occur in the zone from which the puck was shot.

Appendix A

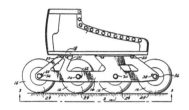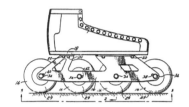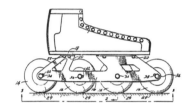

In-line Roller Hockey Leagues

For information on how to join a league and where to play, contact the NIHA.

In the U.S., including Alaska and Hawaii:

National In-line Hockey Association, HQ
P.O. Box 010069
Miami, FL 33101
(305) 358-8988
(800) 358-NIHA
Hours of operation: 8 A.M.–6 P.M.
(Eastern Time)

In Canada:

National In-line Hockey Association, Canada
11810 Kingsway
Edmonton, AB T5G 0X5
(403) 455-NIHA
(800) 668-NIHA
Hours of operation: 9 A.M.–5 P.M.
(Mountain Time)

APPENDIX B

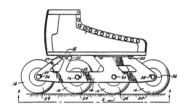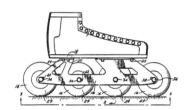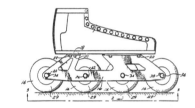

ORGANIZATIONS AND ASSOCIATIONS

Amateur Athletic Union of the U.S.
3400 West 86th Street
P.O. Box 68207
Indianapolis, IN 46268
(317) 872-2900

ASHI
American Street Hockey Institute
P.O. Box 550
Wichendon Springs, MA 01477
(508) 297-0801

CHA
Canadian Hockey Association
1600 James Naismith Drive

Glouchester, ON K1B 5N4
Canada
(613) 748-5617
Fax: (613) 748-5709

Hockey Hall of Fame
Exhibition Place
Toronto, ON M6K 3C3
Canada
(416) 595-1345

IBDHA
International Ball & Deck Hockey Association
1100 East Hector Street, #169

Conshocken, PA 19428
(215) 825-7505

IDTA
International Dekhockey Tournament Association
P.O. Box 1066
Leominster, MA 01453
(508) 537-6711

IISA
International In-Line Skating Association
P.O. Box 15482
Atlanta, GA 30333
(404) 728-9707

National Museum of Roller Skating
P.O. Box 6579
4730 South Street
Lincoln, NE 68506-0579
(402) 483-7551

NDA
National Dekhockey Association
Mill Circle
Winchendon Springs, MA 01477
(508) 297-0089

NHL
National Hockey League
1155 Metcalfe Street, Suite 960
Montreal, PQ H3B 2W2
Canada
(514) 288-9220

NIHA CANADA
National In-Line Hockey Association
11810 Kingsway
Edmonton, AB T5G 0X5
(403) 455-NIHA
(800) 668-NIHA (in Canada)

NIHA World Headquarters
National In-Line Hockey Association

999 Brickell Avenue, Ninth Floor
Miami, FL 33131
(800) 358-NIHA
(305) 358-8988

NIRSA
National Intramural-Recreational
Sports Association
850 SW 15th Street
Corvallis, OR 97333-4145
(503) 737-2088
Fax: (503) 737-2026

NRPA
National Recreation and Parks Association
2775 South Quincy, Suite 300
Arlington, VA 22206
(800) 626-6772
Fax: (703) 671-6772

NYSCA
National Youth Sports Coaches Association
2611 Old Okeechobee Road
West Palm Beach, FL 33409
(407) 684-1141
(800) 729-2057

RSA
Roller Skating Associations
7301 Georgetown Road, Suite 123
Indianapolis, IN 46268
(317) 875-3390

U.S. Olympic Committee
1750 East Boulder Street
Colorado Springs, CO 80909
(719) 632-5551

USA Dekhockey
2120 Mt. Troy Road
Pittsburgh, PA 15212
(412) 231-0151

Association, the Roller Skating Manufacturers, the Society of Roller Skating Teachers of America, the Speed Coaches Association, the Roller Hockey Coaches Association, and the Proficiency Judges.

RSROA. Roller Skating Rink Operators Association. The original parent organization of the United States Amateur Confederation of Roller Skating.

Rush. An individual or combined attack by a team in possession of the puck toward the attacking zone.

S

Scooting. A skating motion, consisting of short thrusts, used in confined areas.

Scramble. A term used to describe the confusion that results when a number of players attempt to gain control of a loose puck.

Screen. A player who blocks the goal-keeper's view of the puck.

Shadowing. The act of closely guarding one specific player.

Shooting Angle. A shooter's position on the playing surface in relation to the goal mouth.

Shoot-Out. A one-on-one matchup between skaters and opposing goalies in which a skater takes the puck from the center face-off spot and moves toward the goalkeeper in an attempt to score a goal. A shoot-out is used to break ties in tournament or playoff games following an overtime period.

Shorthanded. A term used to describe a team playing with fewer skaters than its opponent.

Shot on Goal. A shot made in the direction of the goal.

Shovel Pass. See *Push Pass.*

Skate Save. A save made by a goalkeeper with the skate wheels or boot of the skate.

Slap Shot. A quick, hard shot made by drawing the stick back high above the shoulder, then pulling down and driving through the puck with full force and high follow-through to give the puck power and speed.

Slashing. Hitting, or attempting to hit, another player with a stick. A player found to be slashing will be penalized.

SLC. State league coordinator. An NIHA representative responsible for promoting and administering in-line roller hockey activity on a state level. The SLC's Canadian counterpart is the PLC, or provincial league coordinator.

Slide Shot. A shot that is like a push pass.

Slot. The area of the playing surface directly in front of the goal crease between the face-off circles. It is approximately 10 feet wide and 15 feet long.

Smother. A maneuver, usually by the goalkeeper, to stop the puck by falling on it.

Snap Pass. A quick pass made by moving the stick with a snap of the wrists.

Snap Shot. A shot similar to the slap shot but with the stick coming back only one half or one quarter the distance it does in the slap shot.

Snell. Refers to the Snell Memorial Foundation, an organization that, like ANSI, develops standards for protective equipment. Headquartered in St. James, New York, it is named after race car driver Pete Snell, who was killed in a car crash in the 1950s while wearing a helmet that was more decorative than functional. Snell certification stickers are green or blue and bear a serial number.

Solo. A rush by a player without the assistance of his teammates.

Spearing. Action of poking or attempting to poke an opponent with the toe/point of the stick blade with one or both hands. This is illegal under NIHA rules of play.

Split. The action of the goaltender when he goes down to the playing surface to make a kick save.

Split Vision. The ability to look straight ahead and yet see players on either side and the puck on one's stick.

Splitting the Defense. A puck carrier breaking through two defending players.

Spot Pass. A pass to a spot, rather than to a player, in the expectation that a teammate will arrive at the spot and receive the pass.

Stalling. Delaying the game—by, for example, intentionally shooting the puck over the boards. Illegal under NIHA rules of play.

Stand-Up Goalie. A goalkeeper who attempts to stop most shots while standing up, rather than by dropping to the ice.

Starts and Stops. A common skating drill.

Stick Blade. The wide, flat, sometimes curved wooden part of the stick at the bottom of the shaft. The puck is shot and passed with the stick blade.

Stick Lie. See *Lie*.

Stick Mitt. See *Blocker Mitt*.

Stick Save. A save made by the goalkeeper using the stick.

Stick Shaft. The handle of the stick, extending from the blade to the knob. Although often made of wood, it can also be made of hollow aluminum or a metal composite.

Support Strap. An additional skate buckle used to tighten the cuff (the top of the skate boot).

Sweep Check. A sweeping motion of a stick flat on the playing surface to take the puck away from an opponent.

T

Team Official. Coach, league manager, trainer, and so forth.

Telegraphing. Looking directly at a teammate before passing the puck, or signaling your intentions in any way.

Tip-In. Placing of the stick blade in the path of a puck, thus deflecting or redirecting it into the goal.

Toe Save. A save made by a goalkeeper with the tip of an outstretched skate.

Trailing. The act of following a play, without being directly involved in the play.

U

USA Hockey. The governing body of amateur ice hockey. Formerly *AHAUS*.

USAC/RS. United States Amateur Confederation of Roller Skating. Founded in 1937 as part of the *RSROA*. The national governing body for all roller-skating activities.

USOC. United States Olympic Committee.

W

Waffle Mitt. See *Blocker Mitt*.

Warm-Up. A session prior to the start of a game during which the players stretch and help the goalkeeper prepare for the game.

Wooden Shaft. A stick made of wood. The wooden shaft is permanently attached to the stick blade.

Wraparound. 1) A hard shot made into the attack zone along the boards. The momentum of the shot wraps the puck around and behind the goal and into the opposite corner, where it is met by another player. 2) An attempt to score by coming out from behind the goal and sweeping the puck into the net.

WRHL. World Roller Hockey League. Merged with Roller Hockey International (RHI) in 1993.

Wrist Shot. A quick shot using wrist strength to snap the puck.

Z

Zero Tolerance. An in-line hockey rule forbidding the use of profane language.

Zone. Any of three areas on the playing surface: the attack zone, the neutral zone, and the defensive zone.

Zone Clear. Shooting the puck from one end of the surface to the other in an effort to get it out of the zone quickly. If the puck crosses the goal line, it is a violation, and a face-off will occur in the zone from which the puck was shot.

USAC/RS
United States Amateur Confederation of
Roller Skating
4730 South Street
Lincoln, NE 68506
(402) 483-7551

National Hockey League
Western Conference
Pacific Division

Calgary Flames
Olympic Saddledome
Calgary, AB T2P 3B9
Canada
(403) 261-0475
Fax: (403) 261-0470
Capacity: 20,230
Founded: 6-15-93

Edmonton Oilers
Northlands Coliseum
Edmonton, AB T5B 4M9
Canada
(403) 474-8561
Fax: (403) 477-9625
Capacity: 17,503
Founded: 6-22-79

Los Angeles Kings
The Great Western Forum
3900 West Manchester Boulevard
Inglewood, CA 90308
(310) 419-3160
Fax: (310) 673-8927
Capacity: 16,005
Founded: 6-5-67

San Jose Sharks
San Jose Arena
525 West Santa Clara Street

San Jose, CA 95113
(408) 287-7070
Fax: (408) 999-5797
Capacity: 17,310
Founded: 5-9-90

Vancouver Canucks
Pacific Coliseum
100 North Renfrew Street
Vancouver, BC V5K 3N
Canada
(604) 254-5141
Fax: (604) 251-5123
Capacity: 16,150
Founded: 5-22-70

Central Division

Chicago Blackhawks
United Center
1900 West Madison Street
Chicago, IL 60612
(312) 455-4500
Fax: (312) 455-4511
Capacity: 20,500
Founded: 8-29-94

Dallas Stars
Reunion Arena
901 Main Street, Suite 2301
Dallas, TX 75202
(217) 712-2890
Fax: (214) 712-2800
Capacity: 16,814
Founded: 6-15-67

Detroit Red Wings
600 Civic Center Drive
Detroit, MI 48226
(313) 396-7544
Fax: (313) 567-0296
Capacity: 19,275
Founded: 9-25-26

188 In-Line Roller Hockey

St. Louis Blues
Kiel Center
1401 Clark Street
St. Louis, MO 63103
(314) 622-2500
Fax: (314) 622-2582
Capacity: 17,188
Founded: 6-5-67

Toronto Maple Leafs
Maple Leaf Gardens
60 Carlton Street
Toronto, ON M5B 1L1
Canada
(416) 977-1641
Fax: (416) 977-5364
Capacity: 15,842
Founded: 11-22-17

Winnipeg Jets
Winnipeg Arena
15-1430 Maroons Road
Winnipeg, MN R3G 0L5
Canada
(204) 982-5387
Fax: (204) 788-4668
Capacity: 15,393
Founded: 6-22-79

Eastern Conference

Northeast Division

Boston Bruins
Boston Garden
150 Causeway Street
Boston, MA 02114
(617) 227-3206
Fax: (617) 523-7184
Capacity: 14,448
Founded: 11-1-24

Buffalo Sabres
Memorial Auditorium

Buffalo, NY 14202
(716) 856-7300
Fax: (716) 856-2104
Capacity: 16,284
Founded: 5-22-70

Hartford Whalers
Hartford Civic Center
242 Trumbull Street, Eighth Floor
Hartford, CT 06103
(203) 728-3366
Fax: (203) 522-7707
Capacity: 15,635
Founded: 6-22-79

Montreal Canadiens
Montreal Forum
2313 St. Catharine Street West
Montreal, PQ H3H 1N2
Canada
(514) 932-2582
Fax: (514) 932-8736
Capacity: 17,950
Founded: 11-22-17

Ottawa Senators
Ottawa Civic Centre
300 Moodie Drive, Suite 200
Nepean, ON K2H 9C4
Canada
(613) 721-0115
Fax: (613) 726-1419
Capacity: 10,585
Founded: 12-16-91

Pittsburgh Penguins
Civic Arena
Pittsburgh, PA 15219
(412) 642-1800
Fax: (412) 642-1859
Capacity: 17,537
Founded: 6-5-67

Quebec Nordiques
Colisée de Quebec
2505 Avenue de Colisée
Quebec City, PQ G1L 4W7
Canada
(418) 529-8441
Fax: (418) 529-1052
Capacity: 15,399
Founded: 6-22-79

Atlantic Division

Florida Panthers
Miami Arena
100 North East Third Avenue, Tenth Floor
Ft. Lauderdale, FL 33301
(305) 768-1900
Fax: (305) 768-1920
Capacity: 14,500
Founded: 6-14-93

New Jersey Devils
Meadowlands Arena
East Rutherford, NJ 07073
(201) 935-6050
Fax: (201) 935-2127
Capacity: 19,040
Founded: 6-20-82

New York Islanders
Nassau Veterans' Memorial Coliseum
Uniondale, NY 11553
(516) 794-4100
Fax: (516) 542-9348
Capacity: 16,297
Founded: 6-6-72

New York Rangers
Madison Square Garden
4 Pennsylvania Plaza
New York, NY 10001
(212) 465-6000
Fax: (212) 465-6494
Capacity: 18,200
Founded: 5-15-26

Philadelphia Flyers
The Spectrum
Pattison Place
Philadelphia, PA 19148
(215) 465-4500
Fax: (215) 389-9403
Capacity: 17,380
Founded: 6-5-67

Tampa Bay Lightning
ThunderDome
501 East Kennedy Boulevard, Suite 175
Tampa, FL 33602
(813) 229-2658
Fax: (813) 229-3350
Capacity: 28,000
Founded: 12-16-91

Washington Capitals
US Air Arena
1 Harry S. Truman Drive
Landover, MD 20785
(301) 386-7000
Fax: (301) 386-7012
Capacity: 18,130
Founded: 6-11-74

APPENDIX C

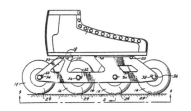 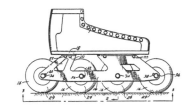 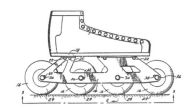

MANUFACTURERS

Each of the following entries is coded by product/service type.

KEY:

SK = Skates
ST = Sticks (hockey)
BR = Bearings
PR = Protective Gear and Accessories
PK = Pucks/Balls
AC = Accessories (clothing, tools,
    individual components)
WH = Wheels
FR = Frames
SH = Shoes
SR = Services
RK = Rink Equipment

Aggro Sport
2125 San Joaquin Hills Road
Newport Beach, CA 92660
(714) 644-9477
(800) 644-9477
Fax: (714) 644-7500
PR, AC

American Sports Data, Inc.
234 North Central Avenue
Hartdale, NY 10530
(914) 328-8877
SR

Andiamo
P.O. Box 1657
Sun Valley, ID 83353
(208) 726-1385
Fax: (208) 726-1388
AC, PR

Arrow Puck
12881 Wheeler Place
Santa Ana, CA 92705
(714) 532-4452
PK

Austin Sportgear
621 Liberty Street
Jackson, MI 49203
(517) 784-1120
AC, PR

Bauer, Canstar Sports USA, Inc.
50 Jonergin Drive
P.O. Box 716
Swanton, VT 05488
(802) 868-2711
Fax: (802) 868-3789
SK, ST, PR, AC

Bell Helmets
(800) 776-5677
PR

Black Hole Performance
P.O. Box 20
Mercer Island, WA 98040
(206) 236-4500
(800) 327-9393
Fax: (206) 236-5490
BR

Blade Tech Corp.
3031 Columbia New Castle Road
New Middletown, OH 44442
(800) 238-2858
AC

BNQ Accessories
Skate Totes
1541 Ocean Avenue, Suite 200
Santa Monica, CA 90401
(800) 643-1092
AC

Boca Bearing
7040 West Palmetto Park Road, Suite 2304
Boca Raton, FL 33433
(800) 332-3256
(407) 998-0004
Fax: (407) 998-0119
BR

Body Armor, Inc.
4900 Prospectus Drive, Suite 200
Durham, NC 27713
(800) 292-7667
Fax: (919) 544-8238
PR, AC

Bones Bearings
Powell Corp.
30 South La Patera
Santa Barbara, CA 93117
(805) 683-9091
Fax: (805) 964-0511
BR

Border Patrol
In-Line Sport Systems, Inc.
821 Marquette Avenue, Suite 2300
Minneapolis, MN 55402
(800) 809-7465
(612) 342-2337
Fax: (612) 338-2302
RK

Boss Speed Bearings
1280 Bison, Suite B9-513
Newport Beach, CA 92660
BR

Bullzeye Wheels
111 Broadway Avenue
Costa Mesa, CA 92627
(800) 646-9664
Fax: (714) 890-7232
WH

California Pro In-Line Skates
8810 Rehco Road
San Diego, CA 92121
(800) 932-5777
Fax: (619) 597-0776
SK

CCM Sports Maska, Inc.
6375 Picard Street
Hyacinthe, PQ J2S 1H3
Canada
(800) 661-8225
(514) 331-5150
Fax: (514) 773-3335
SK, ST, PR, AC

CCM Sports Maska (Maska US)
Pierson Industrial Park
P.O. Box 381
Bradford, VT 05033
(800) 451-4600
SK, ST, PR, AC

CDS Detroit
1167 Lakepoint
Grosse Pointe Park, MI 48230
(313) 331-7371
Fax: (313) 331-7371
AC

Christian Brothers, Inc.
P.O. Box C
Warroad, MN 56763
(218) 386-1111
(800) 867-0847
AC

Core Speed Wheels
2554 Lincoln Boulevard, Suite 244
Venice, CA 90291-5082
(310) 574-8110
Fax: (310) 574-8108
WH

Cyko
316 East Seventh Street, N
P.O. Box 926
Newton, IA 50208
(800) 432-8356
WH

Easton Sports
577 Airport Boulevard
Burlingame, CA 94010
(415) 347-3900
(415) 347-5032
SK

Elec Cell
P.O. Box 160446
Cupertino, CA 95014
(415) 326-6036
AC, PR

Euroglide Slideboards
17091 Daimler
Irvine, CA 92714
(800) 757-5433
AC

Excelsior In-line Frames
607 Atlantic Avenue
Fort Pierce, FL 34950
(800) 942-6805
(407) 465-1162
FR

Exel Marketing, Inc.
Roces Skates
One Second Street
Peabody, MA 01930
(800) 343-5200
SK

Falcon Sports
817 Cedar Falls Road
Menomonie, WI 54751
(715) 235-8830
Fax: (715) 235-8875
ST, AC

First Team Sports, Ultra Wheels
2274 Woodale Drive
Mounds View, MN 55112-4900
(612) 780-4454
(800) 458-2250
Fax: (612) 780-4454
SK, ST, PR, AC

Fitmax
150 Mitchell Boulevard
San Raphael, CA 94903
(800) 786-7779
(415) 499-0841
Fax: (415) 472-5540
PR, AC

Fitness Fanatics
710 Fiero Lane, Suite 17
San Luis Obispo, CA 93401
(805) 547-1030
Fax: (805) 547-9785
FR

Franklin Sports Industries, Inc.
101 Arch Street
Boston, MA 02110
(617) 737-6884
(800) 225-8647
ST, PR, PK, AC

GEM, Inc.
EZ Glide Extreme Axles
2300 Parkwoods Road
Minneapolis, MN 55416
(612) 928-9076
AC

Global Bearings, Inc.
3824 South 79th East Avenue
Tulsa, OK 74145-3232
(800) 331-8020
Fax: (918) 664-1467
BR

Goal-Eez Sports Nets Corp.
2586 Dunwin Drive, Unit 1
Mississauga, ON L5L 1J5
Canada
(416) 820-2499
(416) 820-5142
RK

Grind Zone Skates
P.O. Box 524
Albertville, AL 35950
(800) 322-3851
(205) 878-7619
AC

Grip In-line Speed Control Inc.
5375 Western Avenue, Suite D-1
Boulder, CO 80301
(800) 510-4747
AC

Grizzly Gear
5612 International Parkway
New Hope, MN 55428
(612) 535-2035
WH

Hove Martin Systems, Inc.
112 Bushmills Square
Scarborough, ON M1V 1J4
Canada
(416) 292-9221
SR

Hyper Wheels
15241 Transistor Lane
Huntington Beach, CA 92649
(714) 373-3300
Fax: (714) 373-2525
WH

ICU Skate Company
79 SW First Street
Portland, OR 97209
(503) 497-9083
SK

In-line Sport Systems, Inc.
Border Patrol
821 Marquette Avenue, Suite 2300
Minneapolis, MN 55402
(800) 809-RINK
(612) 342-2337
Fax: (612) 338-2302
RK, AC

In-line Wear
1223 Wilshire Boulevard, Suite 669
Santa Monica, CA 90403
(310) 319-3430
Fax: (310) 319-1572

Itech/FaceShields
c/o Robin Burns Enterprises
RT 104 A, RD #2, Box 1253
P.O. Box 309
Arrowhead Industrial Park
Fairfax, VT 05454
(514) 421-0224
PR

Itech/FaceShields
I-TECH Sports Products Inc.
87B Boul. Brunswick
Dollard de Ormeaux, PQ H9B 2J5
Canada
PR

JetNet Corporation
P.O. Box 8370
Fort Wayne, IN 46898
(800) 953-8638
RK

K2
Exotech Corp.
19215 Vashon Highway SW
Vashon, WA 98070
(206) 463-8145
SK, PR

Karhu, U.S.A., Inc.
Koho/Jofa
P.O. Box 4249
Burlington, VT 05406
(800) 359-3050
(802) 864-4519
Fax: (802) 860-6781
SK, ST, PR, AC

Kneedspeed
2200-4 N.W. Birdsdale
Greesham, OR 97030
(800) 523-7674
(503) 666-9275
Fax: (503) 661-4298
AC

Kryptonics, Inc.
740 South Pierce Avenue
Louisville, CO 80027
(303) 665-5353 x134
(800) 766-9146
Fax: (303) 665-1318
WH

Kuzak Wheels
171 Pier Avenue, Suite 357
Santa Monica, CA 90405
(310) 594-8398
Fax: (310) 594-8398
WH

Labeda
18650 Collier Avenue, Unit A
Lake Elsinore, CA 92530
(217) 324-3961
Fax: (217) 324-2213
WH

Louisville
Hillerick & Bradsby of Canada
14 Arnold Street
Wallaceburg, ON N8A 3P4
Canada
(800) 265-0525
(519) 267-0522
ST, PR, AC

LT Helmets
1275A Vapor Trail
Colorado Springs, CO 80916
(719) 637-0010
Fax: (719) 637-1426
PR

Mateflex
1712 Erie Street
Utica, NY 13501
(800) 926-3539
(315) 733-4600
RK

MDC
Anti-Pollution Mask
6520 California Street
San Francisco, CA 94121
(415) 752-3200
Fax: (415) 752-3777
AC

Mearthane Products Corporation
RollerEdge
16 Western Industrial Drive
Cranston, RI 02921
(401) 946-4400
Fax: (401) 943-8210
WH

Mission Hockey
2981 West McArthir Boulevard, Suite 213
Santa Ana, CA 92704
(714) 556-8856
SK

Mylec, Inc.
Mill Circle Road
Winchendon Springs, VT 05033
(508) 297-0089
Fax: (508) 297-1359
ST, PR, RK, PK, AC

N.Z. Manufacturing, Inc.
6644 South 196th Place
Kent, WA 98032
(206) 251-1485
Fax: (206) 251-0934
AC

Oxygen
9 Columbia Drive
Amherst, NJ 03031
Fax: (800) 258-5020
SK, PR

Paragon Racing Products
690 Industrial Circle S
Shakopee, MN 55379
(800) 328-4827
(612) 496-0091
Fax: (612) 496-0191
AC

Projoy
530 Governors Road
Guelph, ON N1K 1E3
Canada
(800) 387-9499
(519) 821-9444
AC

ProLine Covers
P.O. Box 266
Verdugo City, CA 91046-0266
(818) 541-1736
Fax: (818) 541-0635
AC

Pro-Tec/Helmets
58662 194th Street
Kent, WA 98032
(206) 872-3300
Fax: (206) 872-3267
PR, AC

Respro Products
Anti-Pollution Mask
11203 63rd Street
Edmonton, AB T5W 4E5
Canada
(403) 448-0393
(800) 473-7776
Fax: (403) 448-9044
AC

Riedell Shoes, Inc.
122 Cannon River Avenue
Red Wing, MN 55066
(612) 388-8251
Fax: (612) 388-8616
SH

Rike Inline, Inc.
P.O. Box 1486
Jamestown, NC 27282
(800) 454-5560
FR

Roller Derby Skate Corporation
311 West Edwards Street
Litchfield, IL 62056
(217) 324-3961
SK, AC

Roller Edge Products Corp.
16 Western Industrial Drive
Cranston, RI 02921
(800) 757-3343
(401) 943-8210
WH

Roller Sparks
P.O. Box 919
Cathedral Station
New York, NY 10025
(800) 772-7539
AC

Rollerblade, Inc.
5101 Shady Oak Road
Minneapolis, MN 55343
(800) 232-ROLL
(612) 930-7109
Fax: (612) 930-7030
SK, ST, PR, AC

Rollergrips
765A Loma Verde Avenue
Palo Alto, CA 94303
(415) 493-1117
Fax: (415) 424-0950
AC

Sayre Enterprises
Reflective Products
P.O. Box 1346
Lexington, VA 24450
(800) 552-6064
(703) 463-2768
Fax: (703) 463-2058
AC

Seneca Sports, Inc.
75 Fortune Boulevard
P.O. Box 719
Milford, MA 01757
(508) 634-3616
Fax: (508) 634-8154
SK, ST, PR, AC, PK, RK

Shield
425 Fillmore Avenue
Tonawanda, NY 14150
(800) 828-7669
ST

Shock Doctor
Mouth Guards
EZ Guard Industries
9300 51st Avenue North
Minneapolis, MN 55428
(800) 328-4827 x4018
(612) 537-8400
Fax: (612) 537-5015
AC, PR

Shot Maker
P.O. Box 885
Baudette, MN 55623
(800) 634-6627
RK

The Skate Surgeon Repair
3120 Ryan Drive
Escondido, CA 92025
(619) 480-4477
SR

Sonic Sports, Inc.
10573 West Pico Boulevard
Los Angeles, CA 90064
(310) 558-1830
Fax: (310) 838-3860
AC

Sport Court, Inc.
1075 South 700 West
Salt Lake City, UT 84104
(801) 972-0260
Fax: (801) 975-7752
RK

Stratadrome
IPI
P.O. Box 9601
Colorado Springs, CO 80932
(800) 824-1633
RK

Street Smart
424 New Road
Southhampton, PA 18966-1040
Fax: (609) 983-5585
SK, PR, AC

Strut Specialties
2982 North Cleveland Avenue
Roseville, MN 56113
(612) 628-0688
(612) 628-0788
FR

Sun Hockey
Pentagon Towers
Edina, MN 55435
(800) 933-7825

SureGrip International
5519 Rawlings Street
South Gate, CA 90280
(310) 923-0724
Fax: (310) 923-1160
FR

Team Logos To Go
(818) 998-8572
Fax: (818) 998-0725
SR

Thunderwear
1060-C Calle Negocio
San Clemente, CA
(714) 492-1141
(800) 422-6565
Fax: (714) 492-3259
PR, AC

TKR
SkateStand
P.O. Box 1322
High Point, NC 27261
(919) 882-3226
AC

Tour Con
P.O. Box 930
Litchfield, IL 62056
(217) 324-3961
Fax: (217) 324-2213
PR

Tweeners
624 Grand Avenue, Suite B
Arroyo Grande, CA 93420
(800) 595-4625
RK

Twincam Bearings
Twincam Precision In-line Components
1123 Riverside Drive
Broomsdale, MN 55337
(800) 238-9457
(612) 890-6368
BR

Unitec
Scoreboards
P.O. Box 277
Washington Mills, NY 13479
(800) 383-6060
(315) 736-3967
Fax: (315) 736-4058
RK

US Amateur
Discount Travel
275 East Avenue
Norwalk, CT 06855-9989
(800) 872-1994
SR

The Van Buren Co.
730 West Portland Street
Phoenix, AZ 85007
(800) 869-8981
Fax: (602) 253-9511

Viceroy
Miller & Walker
1655 Gupon Street
Toronto, ON M6P 3T1
Canada
(416) 365-7818
PK

Wigwam Mills, Inc.
3402 Crocker Avenue
P.O. Box 818
Sheboygan, WI 53082-0818
(414) 457-5551
(800) 558-7760
Fax: (414) 457-0311
AC

Yak Research
Slideboards
850 West MacArthur
Oakland, CA 94608
(800) 488-9257
Fax: (510) 652-0893
AC, WH

Zandstra Sports
Postbus 150
Joure, 8500
Netherlands
031-5138-15858
Fax: 031-5138-16415
SK

Zepter Sports International
12780 High Bluff Drive, Suite 200
P.O. Box 261506
San Diego, CA 92196
(619) 530-0844
Fax: (619) 530-2083
AC

Appendix D

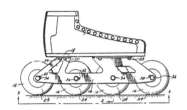 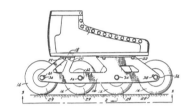 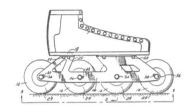

For More Information

Periodicals

Action Sports Retailer
Editor: Brad Bonhall
31652 Second Avenue
South Laguna, CA 92677-3167
(714) 499-4591
Fax: NA
Frequency per year: 12 x
Subscription: NA
Founded: 1980
Description: For retailers of goods and
sportswear in surf, ski, skate, sailboard, and
related product areas.

American Hockey Magazine
Editor: Daryl Seibel
The Publishing Group

1200 North Seventh Street
Minneapolis, MN 55411-4000
(612) 881-3183
Fax: (612) 881-2172
Frequency per year: 9 ×
Subscription: US $12.00
Founded: 1973
Description: Formerly *American Hockey and
Arena* magazine; for those involved in ice hockey
at all levels across America.

ASTM Standardization News
Editor: Barbara Schindler
ASTM
1916 Race Street
Philadelphia, PA 19103-1180
(215) 299-5585
Fax: (215) 977-9679

Frequency per year: 12 ×
Subscription: US $18.00
Founded: 1921
Description: Reports events in materials research, development, and testing.

Athletic Business
Editor: Sue Schmid
1846 Hoffman Street
Madison, WI 53704-2585
(608) 249-0186
Fax: (608) 249-1153
Frequency per year: 12 ×
Subscription: NA
Founded: 1976
Description: Covers athletics, recreation and fitness, facility planning and operation, program management, financing, fund-raising, and equipment purchasing.

Athletic Management
Editor: Sarah Ploss
438 West State Street
Ithaca, NY 14850-5220
(607) 272-0265
Fax: NA
Frequency per year: 6 ×
Subscription: Free
Founded: 1988
Description: Formerly *College Athletics Management*; serves athletic departments at colleges, universities, and high schools nationwide.

Blades On Ice
Editor: Gerri Walbert
7040 North Mona Lisa Road
Tucson, AZ 85741-2633
(602) 575-1747
Fax: (602) 575-1484
Frequency per year: 6 ×
Subscription: US $25.00

Founded: NA
Description: News and information on the ice-skating scene.

California CitySports Magazine
Editor: Jake Steinman
City Sports Publishing Co.
2201 Third Street
San Francisco, CA 94107
(415) 626-1600
Fax: (415) 621-2323
Frequency per year: 12 ×
Subscription: US $18.00
Founded: 1974
Description: Formerly *City Sports* magazine; covers active lifestyles, including participant sports.

Canadian Hockey Magazine
Editor: Phil Legault
Canadian Hockey Association
1600 James Naismith Drive S-607
Gloucester, ON K1B 5N4
Canada
(613) 748-5613
Fax: NA
Frequency per year: 1 ×
Subscription: $4.00
Founded: 1977
Description: Annual covering the sport of amateur ice hockey.

City Fitness
Editor: Tim Brookover
P.O. Box 5009, #108
Houston, TX 77487-5009
(713) 265-9499
Fax: (713) 265-8629
Frequency per year: 12 ×
Subscription: US $18.00
Founded: 1992
Description: For sports and fitness enthusiasts in the Houston area.

Daily Bread
Editor: Angie Walton
P.O. Box 4394
Long Beach, CA 92652
(714) 497-2636
Fax: (714) 497-2636
Frequency per year: 6 ×
Subscription: US $2.95/issue
Founded: 1994
Description: An irreverent 'zine covering the skate scene, with special emphasis on street skating.

Faceoff
Editor: Shawn Coates
1465 St. James Street
Winnipeg, MB R3H 0W9
Canada
(204) 949-6100
Fax: (204) 949-6122
Frequency per year: 7 ×
Subscription: NA
Founded: 1992
Description: Reports on professional ice hockey.

Faceoff: New England's Hockey
Editor: Robert McKenna
Faceoff Sports, Inc.
10 Thompson Square
Boston, MA 02129-3316
(617) 242-9800
Fax: NA
Frequency per year: 12 ×
Subscription: US $18.00
Founded: 1991
Description: Provocative and controversial publications for all hockey aficionados.

Florida Sports
Editor: Mike Woodman
Woodman Publishing
P.O. Box 0897
Miami, FL 33233-0897

(305) 265-0060
Fax: (305) 663-2640
Frequency per year: 10 ×
Subscription: US $15.00
Founded: 1987
Description: Covers a wide variety of sports. Also sports medicine, training, and events calendar.

The Fischler Report
Managing Editor: Shirley Fischler
Fischler Sports Service
520 West 110th Street, #10C
New York, NY 10025
(212) 749-4152
Frequency per year: 52 ×
Subscription: US $480.00
Founded: NA
Description: Covers professional ice hockey. News, trends, and gossip. Exclusive agents' column.

Hockey Atlas
Editor: Phil Stanyer
Atlas Sports, Inc.
3207-275A Street
Aldergrove, BC V4W 3J5
Canada
(604) 730-1319
Fax: (604) 244-9312
Frequency per year: 1 ×
Subscription: US $4.95
Founded: NA
Description: Annual covering ice and roller hockey.

Hockey Digest
Editor: Vince Aversano
Century Publishing, Inc
990 Grove Street
Evanston, IL 60201-4370
(708) 491-6440
Fax: (708) 491-0459

Frequency per year: 8 ×
Subscription: US $12.00
Founded: 1972
Description: Detailed information on the NHL.

Hockey Illustrated
Editor: Stephen Ciacciarelli
Sterling/Macfadden
233 Park Avenue South
New York, NY 10003
(212) 979-4800
Fax: (212) 979-7342
Frequency per year: 4 ×
Subscription: US $12.00
Founded: 1960
Description: A fanzine for the National Hockey League.

Hockey Magazine
Editor: Jess Myers
The Publishing Group
1200 Seventh Street
Minneapolis, MN 55411-4000
(612) 881-3183
Fax: (612) 881-2172
Frequency per year: 7 ×
Subscription: US $18.00
Founded: 1988
Description: Focuses on hockey teams, players, and those connected with the sport. Features, columns, and profiles.

Hockey News
Editor: Steve Dryden
Transcontinental Publishers
85 Scarsdale Road #100
Dons Mills, ON M3B 2R2
Canada
(416) 445-5702
Fax: (416) 445-0753
Frequency per year: 42 ×
Subscription: US $50.00

Founded: 1947
Description: Covers hockey from the pros to major junior hockey.

Hockey Player
Editor: Alex Carswell
P.O. Box 7494
Van Nuys, CA 91327
(818) 878-9573
Fax: NA
Frequency per year: 10 ×
Subscription: US $15.95
Founded: NA
Description: Covers ice and roller hockey. Publisher also produces *Hockey Player* magazine and *From the Rinks to the Streets . . . For Those Who Play.*

Inline Hockey News
Editor: Richard Graham
1044 Pacific Street, #4
Santa Monica, CA 90405
(310) 392-1505
Fax: (310) 392-1505
Frequency per year: 6 ×
Subscription: US $2.95/issue
Founded: 1995
Description: A consumer-oriented magazine written for the roller-hockey enthusiast.

Inline Magazine
Editor: Natalie Kurylko
P.O. Box 527
Mt. Morris, IL 61054-0527
(303) 440-5111, editorial
(815) 734-1116, subscriptions
Fax: (303) 440-3313
Frequency per year: 6 ×
Subscription: US $29.97
Founded: 1991
Description: Covers most aspects of in-line

skating, including departments on speed, vert, street, and roller hockey. Also news, features, events, and product reviews.

Inline Retailer & Industry News
2025 Pearl Street
Boulder, CO 80302
Editor: Rod Rubino
(303) 440-5111, ext. 692
Fax: (303) 440-3313
Frequency per year: 4 ×
Subscription: NA
Founded: 1992
Description: Covers news and information specific to the business side ("the trade") of the in-line skating industry. Manufacturers, retailers, products, trends.

Let's Play Hockey
Editor: Arnie Hamel
Let's Play Inc.
2721 East 42nd Street
Minneapolis, MN 55406-3061
(612) 729-0023
Fax: (612) 729-0259
Frequency per year: 26 ×
Subscription: US $26.00
Founded: 1972
Description: For amateur hockey players in the U.S. Upper Midwest.

MetroSports Magazine
Editor: Giden Fidelzeit
TateHouse Enterprises, Inc.
695 Washington Street
New York, NY 10014
(212) 627-7040
Fax: (212) 242-3293
Frequency per year: 11 ×
Subscription: US $18.00
Founded: NA
Description: Formerly *CitySports*; covers sporting news in New York and Boston.

NIHA Hockeytalk Magazine
Publisher: Dan Bressler
999 Brickell Avenue, Ninth Floor
Miami, FL 33131
(800) 358-6442
Fax: (305) 358-0046
Frequency per year: 4 ×
Subscription: US $2.95/issue
Founded: 1994
Description: The magazine of the NIHA. Published for the amateur in-line roller hockey player, coach, and league coordinator. News, events, profiles, interviews, product updates.

NIRSA Journal
Editor: Gary Miller
NIRSA
850 SW 15th Street
Corvallis, OR 97333-4145
(503) 737-2088
Fax: (503) 737-2026
Frequency per year: 4 ×
Subscription: US $35.00
Founded: 1977
Description: Facility management and development, sport clubs, instruction, fitness, and outdoor recreation.

Northern California Hockey & Skating
Editor: Reggie Winner
Spotlight Publishing, Inc.
701 J Delong Avenue
Novato, CA 94945
Director of Sales: Kelly Corliss
(415) 898-5414
Fax: (415) 892-6484
Frequency per year: 12 ×
Subscription: US $12.00
Founded: 1994
Description: Covers in-line and ice events.

Oldtimers' Hockey News
Editor: Dave Tatham
Talham Publishing, Inc.
640 Christopher Road
Peterborough, ON K9J 1H4
Canada
(705) 743-2679
Fax: (705) 748-3470
Frequency per year: 8 ×
Subscription: US $10.00
Founded: 1975
Description: Covers oldtimer hockey events
around the world.

On Ice Magazine
P.O. Box 10, Station F
Toronto, ON M4Y 2L4
Canada
(416) 469-4367
Fax: NA
Frequency per year: 4 ×
Subscription: US $12.00
Founded: NA
Description: For adult recreational hockey
players.

Parks and Recreation
Editor: Pamela Leigh
National Recreation and Parks Association
2775 South Quincy Street, Suite 300
Arlington, VA 22206
(703) 820-4940
Fax: (703) 671-6771
Frequency per year: 12 ×
Subscription: US $24.00
Founded: 1903
Description: News on people, programs, and
events and technical advances in park, recreation,
and conservation fields.

Pro Hockey Yearbook
Editor: Jerry Croft
Inside Sports, Inc.

990 Grove Street
Evanston, IL 60201
(708) 491-6440
Fax: (708) 491-0459
Frequency per year: 1 ×
Subscription: NA
Founded: NA
Description: Preview of the pro hockey season.

Referee
Editor: Tom Hammil
Referee Enterprises Inc.
P.O. Box 161
Franksville, WI 53126-0161
(414) 632-8855
Fax: NA
Frequency per year: 12 ×
Subscription: US $30.00
Founded: 1976
Description: Covers sports officiating.

Roller Hockey Magazine
Editor: Richard Graham
12327 Santa Monica, Suite 202
Los Angeles, CA 90025
(310) 442-6660
Fax: (310) 442-6663
Frequency per year: 9 × (effective June 1995)
Subscription: US $15.00
Founded: 1992
Description: Formerly *Street Hockey* magazine.
Covers the world of street and in-line roller
hockey. News, features, skills, product reviews,
directory, events.

Skate
Editor: Caroline Pilkington
Roller Skating Association
7301 Georgetown Road #123
Indianapolis, IN 46268-4157
(402) 489-8811
Fax: (402) 489-9785
Frequency per year: 4 ×

Subscription: $12.00
Founded: 1939
Description: Features news and articles for the younger recreational skater.

Snap Shots
Editor: Chris Stevens
Get In-line! Publishing, Inc.
P.O. Box 641200
San Francisco, CA 94164-1200
(800) 758-2664
Fax: (415) 292-4111
Frequency per year: 4 ×
Subscription: US $16.00
Founded: 1994
Description: Newsletter covering in-line skating and in-line roller hockey. News, commentary, trends.

Speedskating Times
Editor: Lauri Muir
2910 Northeast 11th Avenue
Pompano Beach, FL 33064
(305) 782-5928
Fax: (305) 782-5928
Frequency per year: 8 ×
Subscription: US $15.00
Founded: 1989
Description: Covers international ice and in-line speedskating. News, articles, product reviews, events calendar.

Sport Scene
Editor: Jack Hutslar
North American Youth Sport Institute
4985 Oak Garden Drive
Kernersville, NC 27284-9520
(919) 784-4926
Fax: NA
Frequency per year: 4 ×
Subscription: US $16.00

Founded: 1979
Description: Covers sports, recreation, and fitness for youth.

The Sporting News
Editor: Tom Barnidge
Sporting News Publishing, Inc.
1212 North Lindbergh Boulevard
St. Louis, MO 63132-1704
(314) 997-7111
Fax: (314) 993-7726
Frequency per year: 56 ×
Subscription: US $83.00
Founded: 1886
Description: Covers baseball, football, basketball, and hockey. News, features, and columns.

Sports Illustrated
Editor: Mark Mulvoy
Time, Inc.
1271 Avenue of the Americas
New York, NY 10020-1300
(212) 522-1212
Fax: (212) 522-0426
Frequency per year: 52 ×
Subscription: US $65.00
Founded: 1954
Description: The picture weekly covering the whole world of sports.

Sports Illustrated Canada
Editor: Mark Mulvoy
Time, Inc.
1271 Avenue of the Americas
New York, NY 10020-1300
(212) 522-1212
Fax: (212) 522-0426
Frequency per year: 7 ×
Subscription: NA
Founded: 1993
Description: Canadian sports news and interviews.

Sports Illustrated For Kids
Editor: Mark Mulvoy
Time, Inc.
1271 Avenue of the Americas
New York, NY 10020-1300
(212) 522-1212
Fax: (212) 522-0426
Frequency per year: 12 ×
Subscription: US $18.00
Founded: 1989
Description: Covers sports and activities for youth eight years and up.

US College Hockey Magazine
Editor: Don Cameron
North American Sports Communication
37 Trask Road
Peabody, MA 01960-2738
(508) 531-4311
Fax: NA
Frequency per year: 26 ×
Subscription: US $24.00
Founded: 1979
Description: Covers college hockey.

Women's Sport and Fitness Magazine
Editor: Marjorie McCloy
2025 Pearl Street
Boulder, CO 80302-5323
(303) 440-5111
Fax: (303) 440-3313
Frequency per year: 12 ×
Subscription: US $32.00
Founded: 1974
Description: Covers women in sports. News, features, profiles, product reviews.

Videos

"Winning In-line Hockey"
Produced by Greer & Associates
Minneapolis, MN
Directed by Kenneth Greer
Distributed by In-line Hockey Partners
821 Marquette Avenue, Suite 2312
Minneapolis, MN 55402
(612) 342-2337
Release: 1994
Running Time: 30 minutes
Cost: US $19.95
Description: An upbeat, instructional production featuring Herb Brooks (former NHL coach and coach of the 1980 Olympic gold-medal ice hockey team) and Mike Butters (Roller Hockey International player). Instruction on equipment, passing, shooting, and more.
Endorsed by Rollerblade and the NIHA.

"Coaching Youth In-line Hockey Series"
Produced by the NIHA and the NYSCA
Distributed by National Youth Sports Coaches Association (NYSCA)
2611 Old Okeechobee Road
West Palm Beach, FL 33409
(407) 684-1141
(800) 729-2057
Release: 1994
Running Time: 68 minutes
Cost: Part of Coaches Certification Program
Also available through the NIHA:
(800) 358-NIHA
Description: A joint production between the NIHA and the NYSCA. An instructional video for coaches. NIHA staff take you through a complete in-line roller hockey practice from a coach's perspective. Addresses effective communication, equipment, instructional techniques and drills, and other coaching tools. Part of the NIHA's alliance with the NYSCA's Coaches Certification Program.

Computer On-Line Resources

CompuServe
5000 Arlington Center Boulevard
P.O. Box 20212
Columbus, OH 43220
(800) 848-8990
(614) 457-8650
Basic Membership: US $8.95/month
Description: An on-line service with easy-to-navigate graphic interface. CompuServe has hundreds of special-interest forums where people can meet and read about various subjects or "chat" with other users in real time. "Gateway" to Internet (see below) to launch in 1995.
See the "Health and Fitness Forum" for the in-line skating/roller hockey area.

America On-line
8619 Westwood Center Drive
Vienna, VA 22180
(800) 227-6364
Basic Membership: US $9.95/month (5 free hours)
Description: An on-line service with easy-to-navigate graphic interface. Many interest groups on sports and fitness. Also has a "gateway" to the Internet (see below).

The Internet
It is beyond the scope of this book to go into how to access the Internet, let alone navigate it. The best place to learn more about the Internet is your local bookstore. There are more books published on the Internet than on any other computer field, so you should not have any trouble finding one. Once you get "on-line," tap in to some or all of the following.

Skating
Origins, equipment reviews, technique instructions, maintenance advice, FAQs ("frequently asked questions"), location lists, and much more for in-line skating, in-line roller hockey, roller figure, and speed skating.
Anonymous FTP (File Transfer Protocol):
Address: rtfm.mit.edu
Path: /pub/usenet/news.answers/rec-skate-faq

Sports Articles
Stadium listings, rosters, results, schedules, rules, history, and more about stadium sports.
Anonymous FTP:
Address: rtfm.spies.com
Path: /library/article/sports

Sports Schedules
Easy access to professional football, hockey, basketball, and baseball schedules from a single menu.
Gopher:
Name: Ball State University
Address: gopher.bsu.edu
Choose: Professional Sports Schedules

Sports Statistics
Statistics for football (NFL), hockey (NHL), basketball (NBA), and baseball (MLB).
Anonymous FTP:
Address: wuarchive.wustl.edu
Path: /doc/misc/sports

NHL Schedules
Get the day's game schedule for your favorite NHL hockey teams. Enter help for help. Full schedules are also available.
Telnet:
Address: culine.colorado.edu 860

APPENDIX E

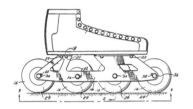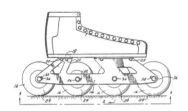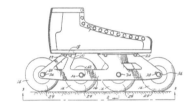

BIBLIOGRAPHY

Alexander, Jeff. "History in the Making." *Street Hockey* magazine (July 1993): 14–17.

Balog, Doug. Interview by author.

Bauer, Seth, ed. "Walking to Fitness." *Walking* magazine. Boston: The Walking Magazine, 1991.

Canstar Sports, Inc. *Bauer Press Kit*. Swanton: Canstar Sports, Inc., 1994.

Coaching Youth In-line Hockey Series. Produced and directed by National Youth Sports Coaches Association, 68 min., videocassette.

"Directory." *Roller Hockey* magazine (Nov. 1994): 62–63.

Hyper In-line. *Hyper In-line Press Kit*. Huntington Beach: Hyper In-line, 1994.

Jones, Shawn M. Interview by author, 1994.

Joyner, Stephen C. *The Joy of Walking: More Than Just Exercise.* Crozett: Betterway Publications, Inc., 1992.

————. *The Complete Guide & Resource to In-line Skating.* Cincinnati: F&W Publications, Inc., 1993.

Karhu U.S.A., Inc. *Street In-line Hockey.* South Burlington: Karhu U.S.A. Inc., 1994.

MacAdam, Don, and Reynolds, Gail. *Hockey Fitness: Year-Round Conditioning On and Off the Ice.* Champaign: Leisure Press, 1988.

Madden, Mark. "Ball Hockey." *Street Hockey* magazine (Feb./March 1993): 39–42.

————. "The NHL and Roller Hockey International." *Street Hockey* magazine (Oct./Nov. 1993): 10–12.

Meagher, John W. *Coaching Hockey: Fundamentals, Team Play and Techniques.* Englewood Cliffs: Prentice-Hall, Inc., 1972.

Mireault, Joseph R. Interview by author, 1994.

Naegele, Robert O., III. Interview by author, 1994.

National In-line Hockey Association. *NIHA Fact Sheet.* Miami: National In-line Hockey Association, 1994.

————. *NIHA Official Rulebook.* Miami: National In-line Hockey Association, 1994.

————. *NIHA Press Kit.* Miami: National In-line Hockey Association, 1994.

National Intramural-Recreational Sports Association. *NIRSA Press Kit.* Corvallis: National Intramural-Recreational Sports Association, 1994.

National Museum of Roller Skating. *Historical Roller Skating Overview.* Lincoln: National Museum of Roller Skating, 1994.

National Youth Sport Coaches Association. *What We're All About . . .* West Palm Beach: National Youth Sport Coaches Association.

The 1994 Information Please Almanac, 47th ed. Boston: Houghton Mifflin, 1994.

Olson, Scott. Interview by author, 1994.

Park, Rod. *Playing Hockey the Professional Way*, 1st ed. New York: Harper & Row, Publishers, 1972.

Rollerblade, Inc. *Rollerblade Press Kit*. Minneapolis: Rollerblade, Inc., 1994.

Schnieder, Ken. "Skate Traits: The Hot, New Skates of '94." *Roller Hockey* magazine (July 1994): 36–39.

Setzer, Mike. "The NHL & Street Hockey." *Street Hockey* magazine (Oct./Nov. 1993): 23–25.

———. "Five Simple Steps to Improve Your Game." *Roller Hockey* magazine (March 1994): 26–27.

Stamm, Laura. *Laura Stamm's Power Skating*, 2nd ed. Champaign: Leisure Press, 1989.

Stanyer, Philip R. *Hockey Atlas*, 1st. ed. Aldergrove, B.C.: Atlas Sports Inc., 1994.

Stout, Rick, and Hahn, Harley. *The Internet Yellow Pages*. New York: Osborne McGraw-Hill, 1994.

Traub, Morris, ed. *Skating Backwards*. "Roller Skating Through the Years: The Story of Roller Skates, Rinks, and Skaters." New York: William-Frederick Press, 1944.

Turner, James. *History of Roller Skating*. Lincoln: Roller Skating Rink Operators Association of America, 1975.

Watt, Tom. *How To Play Hockey: A Guide for Players and Their Coaches*. Toronto: Doubleday Canada Ltd., 1971.

"Winning In-line Hockey." Produced and directed by Greer & Associates, 30 min., 1994, videocassette.

Zuver, Henry. Interview by author, 1994.